Hard to Watch:

The Films of Steven Seagal

Edited by David C. Hayes

Published in the USA by
BearManor Media
1317 Edgewater Dr. #110
Orlando, FL 32804
www.BearManorMedia.com

Softcover Edition
ISBN-10:
ISBN-13: 979-8-88771-012-9

Printed in the United States of America

Dedicated in loving memory to Kevin Moyers.

Introduction

My introduction to Steven Seagal as a young lad was through the magic of VHS tapes. The explosive covers and swashbuckling heroes beckoned to me in my youth… it was portable, within reason, and I could get exactly what I needed in terms of an entertainment fix for a measly $1.99. I rented *Above the Law*, at the tender age of 17, and never looked back. I would remain a Sensei Seagal fan for a number of years after, all the way through the tragically ego-centric roles and acting choices of the 2000s through the dogged determination to reinvent his backstory depending on the interview being conducted. He was an enigma, really. You can call it buffoonery or outright lies, but the fact remains that you never, ever knew what Sensei was going to say or what amazing life event was about to be revealed (or fabricated) at any given moment. There was, and still is, an air of mystery around Seagal and that, in and of itself, is a large part of why he has persisted for so long despite the general lack of real performance talent. Or writing talent. Or directing and producing talent. Shockingly, there is some musical talent, but that is a story for later in this volume.

My fandom survived all of these things but, curiously, it couldn't survive actually dealing with man. Not directly, mind you, but through a series of events and professional obligations, Sensei managed to dim the torch I held for him. That torch held high was something that survived the (sometimes unsubstantiated) stories of Kurt Russell felling Sensei on the set of *Executive Decision* with one blow resulting in Seagal's character being effectively cut from the film. It survived the multiple different interviews where he indicated he was of Sicilian descent, then Jewish descent, then Asian descent, then… you get the picture. It appears Sensei took 23 and Me as a literal number to hit. I didn't care. I didn't care that, in the 21st Century, he painted his widow's peak on. I didn't care that the latter films all involved limited interaction between Sensei and the rest of the cast, often coupled with garbled, guttural, improv dialogue. I could always look back at *Above the Law* or *Hard to Kill* or any of the myriad of "Steven Seagal is…" title preamble films and bask in his glory.

I could see beyond the multiple verified accounts of "Judo" Gene LeBell putting Sensei to sleep and causing him to defecate in his ghee. I didn't even mind the energy drink fiasco, the contention that he actually taught top-level UFC fighters how to kick, or that time that he had that tank in Arizona and accidentally invaded the wrong home while looking for illegal immigrants in Arizona with Joe Arpaio. The staged Russian fight exhibition and Sensei's friendship and unofficial ambassador status with Vladimir Putin. I lasted through all of that.

Then, one day, I was asked to work on a screenplay featuring Sensei. My excitement was palpable and visible. The job would be tough, though: 72-hour turnaround on an action feature, the character of "The General" needed some very specific requirements, including limited screen time, dialogue, a final, rousing monologue, and a scene where a young female character sits on his lap. Got it. I could make all that happen AND it came in on time. Within 24 hours the notes came back. There was another older action star that agreed to come in on the project as the foil to our good guy general. 'Sweet,' I thought. The catch was, these two actors could never be in a scene together due to real life animosity, so the final battle scene would need to be conducted by surrogates. 'Weird,' I thought, 'but O.K.' Who was I to second or third guess members of action movie royalty? Last requirement for this round was the 24-hour turnaround on this revision. I took a deep breath and imagined my name above a title: *David C. Hayes is… Up for the Challenge.* Besides, there was a check coming! I could do it.

And do it I did. There followed one more 24-hour revision with the inclusion of another, more stoic, action star who required his character to be a grocery bagger that comes out of retirement and would function as comic relief. At that point, who cared, right? Sure. Done. Finished.

Then, it went back to the man for approval. From what I understand, the script was fine, but, after working with and talking with and negotiating with the production company, Sensei didn't feel that the director's action reel was to his liking (for the record, it had been that same director that had been working, talking, and negotiating). He pulled the plug on the project, and, in no uncertain terms, he pulled the plug on my unconditional love. There was no warning and no indication that the project was anything but a 'go' from the main man the entire time.

Now, I get it. I understand how Hollywood works (been doing this quite some time), but it never stops hurting. Maybe I expected more? Maybe I thought Nico was really out for justice, or only Ryback could keep that submarine from being under siege, or Forrest Taft really was out to save the planet, even if he did stand on deadly ground.

Or maybe I'm just a bitter old screenwriter that wanted to write a thing because he was a big fan. That's more than likely the case. Oh, and since the deal was dead, so was the payment. Sayonara, token check I agreed to in order to write a Steven Seagal movie.

Sayonara dreams.

Sayonara.

–David C. Hayes

Above the Law (1988)

Movies are about wish fulfillment.

When we go to see movies, we're going to see things we'll never see, do things we'll never be able to do. The majority of people never get into a fist fight in their lives, and when they do they're mostly more uncomfortable than gratifying. Sure, you taught the guy a lesson, but now your fist hurts, there's broken glass in your beard and the bartender is screaming at you to get out of his place. A fist fight isn't a triumphant thing, it's ugly, painful and often pointless. This is why the world of 1988 needed a guy like Steven Segal, and a movie like *Above the Law*.

To say 1988's *Above the Law* is wish fulfilment is a bit reductive. At its core it's a pretty typical action film about an Italian American who learns martial arts, fights in Vietnam, then becomes a Chicago cop only to run afoul of the local drug dealers and the corrupt U.S. government. A tale as old as time, the trope of the tough as nails cop going rogue to do what's right was already old hat by the 1980s. We'd all seen it before. So why was this movie a breakout hit where so many other buddy cop action films flew by with no one remembering? Well, firstly it should be said that this was a really well-made movie. It had relatable characters, a good script, and it was shot very well. By all accounts though, it still should have been pretty forgettable… so why wasn't it forgotten?

Steven Segal.

Look, I know he's a bit of a joke nowadays, but if you're gonna' fall from grace you gotta' start in grace. When this movie was made Segal wasn't an overweight, misogynistic manatee who wore funny outfits and thought he was magic. He was the real deal, he knew how to shoot a gun, knew martial arts, and was perfectly willing to do his own stunts. He arrived on the scene just as *American Martial arts* movies were starting to become cool. His style was a bit different from what had been seen before, instead of kicks and punches his style was smoother, cooler. He was graceful and violent at once. He sold the action scenes in this movie and made them believable and satisfying. What's more, he was handsome, suave and charming. His character had a deep respect for family, and patriotism. He seemed like a guy you could have a beer with; the only people he threatened were the bad guys. Hell, he wore jeans for most of the movie, he was married to Sharon Stone, he had more cool than most of us could hope to achieve in ten lifetimes. If there was a kitten in a tree in this movie, he'd have found the coolest way possible to get it down.

Have you got it yet? Steven Segal was the wish fulfillment in this movie because we all wanted to be that guy. In the first moments of the movie, Nico bears witness to some CIA scumbags torturing innocent Vietnamese civilians. Instead of standing idly by, he busts the guy's nose! With one punch he makes us all feel a little better about the complex geopolitical issues of the Vietnam war. Later, Nico rescues his cousin from a bunch of drug dealers by systematically beating the tar out of all of them. Maybe it's silly but when he grabs the dealer by the hair and smashes his face into a coke mirror while taunting the scumbag "You wanna get high?" he's fighting a very literal war on drugs that he can really win just by doling out a heaping helping of pain. Then a corrupt CIA agent stands in his way and at gunpoint Segal gives him a pointed speech about how corrupt they are, and declares "You think you're above the law? You ain't above mine."

This is probably why it hurts so bad when we see a guy like Segal, who gave us all what we wanted to see become a bloated parody of himself. Truth is, I liked watching this movie again. I enjoyed it with the same wide-eyed wonder that I did when I was a kid. It returned me to a time when there were heroes in the world, and all you had to do to fix the world's problems is punch some bad guys in the face. Sadly, in our real world there's rarely a face to punch. Sure, we all can fight for a better world, but we lack the instant gratification of breaking noses of people who sorely deserve it.

This is wish fulfillment that you can only get in a movie. In real life, atrocities happen in war, drugs rule the streets, and police corruption is rampant. As much as we want to solve these problems with a one-liner and a few aikido movies, we just can't. All these things require a lot of people working very hard, for a very long time to change, and sometimes you just can't fix them. See why movies are better than reality? Steven Segal can't solve the world's problems, but damn it, if it's not fun seeing him represent us all when he beats the tar out of the bad guys.

In the movies a man like Steven Segal is our representative. He's our ideal, he's our symbol. In real life he's a bit of an egotistical jerk but on that screen he's everything we want to see. Life is better up on that silver screen; things always work out for the best and the bad guy always gets what's coming to him. It's a world we all want, a world we all need. Something to strive for at least, and maybe someday make real.

–Joshua Knode

Hard to Kill (1990)

Steven Seagal broke onto the film scene when I was in high school. I remember sitting with some friends and getting high, watching *Above the Law* for the first time. There was something radically different about Seagal. He seemed so relaxed, even when he was fighting. He seemed to exude a coolness unlike anything we'd ever seen. Even the great Bruce Lee became animated and yelled when he fought. But this Seagal guy hardly broke a sweat. I would (briefly) become a fan of Seagal, and *Hard to Kill* would be my favorite. So going back and rewatching it all these years later, I wondered how the movie would hold up. The answer was, well, it sucked. If anything, it serves as a reminder that I had horrendous tastes when I was a younger man. (Maybe it would have enhanced my viewing experience had I been smoking weed while viewing it, but I wasn't, and it sucked like a Hoover vacuum cleaner.)

So yeah, *Hard to Kill* is crap, but Seagal is not the worst thing about it. Not even close. He's not even the worst *Steven* involved with the film. Both of those distinctions go to Steven McKay, the writer behind the film's impressively poor script. (To be fair to McKay, I cannot say for certain that Seagal didn't bully the director, Bruce Malmuth, into making on-set changes. This would not be at all surprising given Seagal's penchant for awfulness.) This will surprise no one, but the first director approached for the film, Craig R. Baxley, passed on the film because he didn't want to work with Seagal. On a related note, Seagal proved himself once again Hard to Work With by making enemies with Malmuth, of whom Seagal said, "I think it's a miracle this guy can put one foot in front of the other."

The film begins with Seagal as a lone cop (with the porn-rific name "Mason Storm") on a dark pier surveilling some bad guys. Thanks to some horrible hiding (literally "hiding in plain sight"), Storm is spotted. He then flees the scene and *immediately* gets into a situation where he must dispatch a band of street toughs trying to rob a bodega (as one does). After making light work of the shotgun-wielding baddies (almost all bad guys in this movie carry shotguns), he goes home and makes sweet, sweet love to his wife. Shortly after the conclusion of the Storms' lovemaking, the bad guys from the pier show up and gun down Storm, his wife, and (supposedly) his son. When Storm's old pal, Internal Affairs detective O'Malley realizes that Storm has been set up by bad cops, he (alone?) convinces everyone that Storm and his family are dead. This entire portion of plot is ridiculous. There is no way O'Malley could have engineered all of this alone. The guy even manages to stage fake funerals. So, unbeknownst to everyone who is not O'Malley, Storm and his son are still alive. Storm spends the next seven years in a coma (who is paying for these medical bills? Is it O'Malley, on his cop's salary?), while O'Malley raises his son as his own.

When Storm finally wakes up in the hospital, he moves around with only limited loss of mobility. Sure, he's creaky and can't immediately walk, but after a few weeks of *Rocky IV*-like outdoors training he will be back to his old self, walking and running with strangely erect posture and snapping and twisting arms and legs willy-nilly. (As someone who spent three weeks in a coma myself, I can assure you this is not even remotely realistic. Even after a mere few weeks, all of my muscles atrophied and I had to learn to walk again. However, I was still able to act better than Seagal, so I suppose it evens out.) The downside of the coma is that Storm missed seven years of his life, but the upside is that he woke up to smoking hot Kelly LeBrock longing to be his woman. (I am sad to report there was no Kelly LeBrock waiting for me when I woke up. But again, I was still a better actor and person than Seagal.) She stays by his side as he hides out, regains his strength, and then goes out to enact revenge. Despite it feeling to Storm like he fell asleep and then woke up the next day to find that his wife is dead, he's not too broken up about it. He doesn't really cry (no doubt Seagal's limited acting would have hampered this) and only a few weeks later he has a pseudo-romantic sex scene with

LeBrock, complete with a dozen lit candles and super corny saxophone music (the score to the entire film is pretty terrible).

Storm discovers that the man who orchestrated his set-up and the murder of his wife is Senator Vernon Trent. After hearing Trent's catchphrase "You can take that to the bank" on a TV ad, Storm utters the film's most (god awful) memorable line: "I'm gonna take you to the bank, Senator Trent. … *The blood bank!*" Pay no attention to the fact that the line makes zero sense. It's badass, right? Well, no, not really, but in the world of Steven Seagal movies, this is what passes for badass.

The film is significant because it features the first appearance of Seagal's greasy ponytail. It also marks one of the earliest film appearances of *Breaking Bad* actor Dean Norris. Adding to the significance, I'm fairly certain Quentin Tarantino found inspiration here for The Bride's coma in the *Kill Bill* films.

As far as Steven Seagal movies go, this one isn't too bad (this is akin to saying "this turd doesn't smell as bad as most turds do"). And despite Seagal's dislike for Bruce Malmuth, the director's work here — *Hard to Kill* feels something like low-rent Jerry Bruckheimer — is one of his better outings.

–Andrew J. Rausch

Marked for Death (1990)

Marked for Death was Steven Seagal's third box office movie. It would seem to be a good choice to watch but, 30 years later, *Marked for Death* has become hard to watch. This doesn't mean there's not a redemptive side to *Marked for Death...*

I've learned to look for the positive in movies as my wife *loves* bad, cheesy movies. It's become a sort of ritual in our household to watch the worst of the worst movies. *Marked for Death* isn't the worst of the worst. It falls somewhere in the middle of the pack for bad movies. That's a good thing. It helped me look at *Marked for Death* through the eye of a leader. This is something I do regularly through my Reel Leadership series (https:// jmlalonde.com/reel-leadership). I want to look at *Marked for Death* through the lens of a leader. It may be a bit different than you're used to reading. Yet, I think you'll have fun with this.

Sometimes you have to get the job done as soon as possible: Steven Seagal's character, John Hatcher, had recently become an undercover agent. He had gone undercover as a drug dealer and was buying crack from a distributor. After the drug dealer asked for the *green,* Hatcher and the dealer decided to do the deal. They begin the exchange after exchanging words telling one another to they wanted to get the deal done as quickly as possible. What can this teach us about leadership? There are times when we do business with someone we don't like or care for. We only want to do the deal. In these situations, it is wise to get the deal done as soon as possible. Make the monetary exchange and get out of there. Don't go back. Don't try to get more business. Just get the job done and go.

Your people will pay the consequences for your decisions: Hatcher's partner, Chico, was hesitant to go to the drug deal. They had recently apprehended another gang member, Hector. Hector's apprehension was messy. There was a chase. There was a fight. It caused a ruckus and many of the citizens had seen what happened. This put a target on Hatcher and Chico. The bad guys may hear that there is law enforcement in the area. If the drug dealer figures out that it was Hatcher and Chico, they would be in danger. And the drug dealers did figure out the rouse Hatcher and Chico had put on. They launched an attack and began firing at the duo. As they tried to make their escaped, one of the women in the building pulled out a gun. She blasted Chico and Hatcher lost his partner. We have to be cautious when we disregard the feelings of those we lead. They have a voice and we need to listen to them. We may not like what they have to say. We may not want to do what they're suggesting… yet, they see and know more than we give them credit for. Make sure you're taking into account what your team members are saying and suggesting. By ignoring their hunches, you're putting them in danger.

You can go too far: *Marked for Death* cuts to Hatcher sitting in a confessional booth. He's confessing his sins to the Catholic priest. And he's confessing to some pretty ugly stuff. Hatcher had gone too far many times in his career. He had done whatever it took to get the bad guy. This meant he would sleep with women to get information. He would do drugs to look legit. He did anything he could to blend in. Leaders can go too far to. They want to make the big deal or land the desired client. To do this, they may be tempted to do something wrong to seal the deal. We've seen this with Enron and other big corporations that fell. You have to be careful how far you go. Know the limits and don't cross the line.

Leaders need to know how to get out of tight spots: The Jamaicans attacked Hatcher as he was driving in his Ford Mustang. They blocked him in using construction equipment. Eventually, they began to crush the Mustang using the bucket of a large front loader. Hatcher was trapped inside the Mustang, underneath the bottom of the bucket. One of the Jamaicans tossed a Molotov cocktail into the crushed car. It's now on fire and Hatcher is in a tight spot. He saw an opening. He began to work his way out of the burning vehicle. He was successful. There are times when we get into a tight spot. We may have made a bad decision or something we thought would work didn't. These are leadership tight spots. We have to be ready to get out of our tight spots in an ethical way.

Great leaders are willing to apologize: Max was the coach at the high school in Lincoln Park, a suburb of Chicago. He saw the damage the Jamaican and Colombian drug trade had done to his city. He was tired. He was angry. He had a prejudice against Jamaicans. Then there was Charles. Charles is a Jamaican that was also part of the Chicago police department. Charles teamed up with Max and Hatcher. But Max wasn't happy with this decision. Max had a hard on against Charles. He believed all Jamaicans were bad. He believed they couldn't be trusted. By the end of *Marked for Death*, Max was offering an apology to Charles. He discovered he had a prejudice against Jamaicans and he wasn't willing to hide it. We all have prejudices. We all have ideas about people we lead and work with. These prejudices are often wrong. When we're wrong, we need to be like Max. We have to be willing to step up and say "I'm sorry. I was wrong. Will you forgive me?" Apologies go a long way. They show people you have grown from a place of wrongness to a place of realization of what is right. Be willing to apologize and say I'm sorry. While *Marked for Death* is hard to watch, it is also a learning tool. You may be surprised what you find in this Steven Seagal flick.

–Joe LaLonde

Saturday Night Live (1991)

Out of all the stars active during the '80s/'90s golden age of action movies, it's hard to imagine one less suited to host Saturday Night Live than Steven Seagal.

It's not simply that he's not funny. It's that he barely seems *human.*

A celebrity doesn't have to be a good comic actor in order to be a good *SNL* host. Hell, a celebrity doesn't have to be an actor of any kind at all. But what they do need, undeniably, is some sense of charm, something that makes you think "yeah, this person might be worth the GDP of a small country, but I bet they'd be fun to get some beers and crack jokes with."

Schwarzenegger, Stallone, Van Damme, Lundgren, and Norris have all done movies where, in between the kickboxing and gunfights, their characters stop long enough to smile, laugh, and just be *real.* Even in his most relaxed moments, though, Seagal's only interests seem to be breaking wrists and appropriating Asian culture. Scenes where he's supposed to play a loving husband or father come off cold and detached. Just try to picture Seagal's character from *Hard to Kill* taking his kid to Chuck E. Cheese; it's horrifying!

It's no surprise then that Seagal's opening monologue for the one and only episode of *SNL* he hosted (April 20, 1991) fails to offer any glimpse into the actor as a real person. It doesn't even allow room for playful self-mockery. It is instead a deadly serious lecture about how modern man has strayed from the warrior path and how U.S. politicians are all corrupt and blah blah blah. Schwarzenegger may have found his greatest fame as a Terminator, but it's Seagal who truly comes off like a robot. Worse yet, he's a *pretentious Zen robot.*

In what is presumably supposed to be a humorous counterweight to this dour diatribe, Seagal's closes his monologue by picking up a guitar and warbling an acoustic version of "Kung-Fu Fighting." Chris Rock is one of several cast members stuck contributing backup vocals and you can tell by the look on his face that he knows this is going to be a long night.

Of course, Seagal's aloofness could be utilized for comic effect if filtered through that trusty comedy filter known as "the straight man." Serving as a po-faced foil to the wacky antics of others, a self-serious straight man can actually amplify a scene's humor by virtue of juxtaposition. The problem, however, is that it's often necessary to position the straight man as the butt of the joke, and Steven Seagal refuses to be the butt of anyone's joke. Ever.

To wit, during the episode's cold open, as Kevin Nealon and Dana Carvey's Austrian bodybuilding duo Hans and Franz extol the virtues of their "cousin" Arnie, Seagal saunters onstage and dismisses his action film competition handily, boasting that unlike Schwarzenegger and the rest, he is truly unique. Hans and Franz are instantly smitten, to the point where they fantasize about sporting slicked-back ponytails, black trenchcoats, and monotone voices just like their new hero.

What happens when the straight man's fame is such that he can refuse to play the straight man? What happens when that same straight man's ego likewise refuses to let him debase himself by playing the fool?

As would be the case when Donald Trump hosted the show in 2015, the result is 90 cringe-inducing minutes of awkward television featuring otherwise skilled comedians being held hostage by the preening narcissism of an oblivious prima donna. Over the years, stories about Seagal's legendarily bad behind-the-scenes behavior have trickled out: verbal abuse, excessive demands, self-serving rewrites, flubbed lines, etc. Norm Macdonald, David Spade, Tim Meadows, and even Lorne Michaels himself have openly referred to Seagal as the worst SNL host they ever worked with.

Unsurprisingly, Seagal was banned from the show after his appearance and reruns of the episode have since been hacked to ribbons in an attempt to edit out the worst of the aikido master's "contributions." Of the five sketches he appears in, the "joke" is almost always the same: Seagal is cool and badass, while everyone around him is a doofus.

When Seagal, playing a rogue police officer demoted to deskwork after kicking too much criminal ass, encounters Rob Schneider's recurring character The Richmeister, it ends with the comedian violently stuffed into a copy machine before being dangled out a window. In another skit, Seagal is a father whose threats to his daughter's deadbeat boyfriend (Chris Farley) get increasingly dire and absurd, but the actor's sluggish, half-whispered delivery kills the whole shtick dead.

The episode-closing sketch plays like an early draft of *On Deadly Ground*, with Seagal as a nature photographer trying to expose an eco-terrorist plot by Phil Hartman's smarmy oil tycoon; it climaxes with Seagal—what else?—beating the crap out of Hartman before turning directly to the camera and warning audiences about the dangers of pollution. No humor. No winking. Just preachiness.

Again and again, some of the funniest talents *SNL* has ever fostered struggle in vain to generate laughs, tripping all over themselves to prop up this humorless, squinty-eyed, self-styled sentinel of machismo and enlightenment. Seagal's sole attempt to be silly and to play a character that isn't basically himself sees him adopting a bad Elvis wig and an exaggerated New Yawk accent in order to brutally skewer Andrew Dice Clay's box office failures.

The audience is painfully silent throughout, thanks largely to Seagal's terrible comic timing, but there is some hilarity in hindsight. Seagal making fun of someone else's cinematic output is rich given that his own stardom wouldn't even survive the end of the decade.

Seagal's mainstream success always had a short shelf life. His limited acting abilities and apathy towards any genre other than action, as well as the fact that aikido is not a showy fighting style, all spelled doom for him in the long run. His biggest flaw, though, might be the one highlighted here: his utter lack of relatability.

Ironically, Steven Seagal's inability to laugh at himself is the reason he became the joke that he is today.

–William Tea

Out for Justice (1991)

Steven Seagal's fourth movie, *Out for Justice*, has acquired the reputation of being one of the finest in the star's oeuvre. In the essential tome *Seagalogy: A Study of the Ass-Kicking Films of Steven Seagal* (2008) author "Vern" calls it a "standout" and concludes his chapter on the film by writing "whenever someone asks me what is the *best* Steve Seagal movie, I tell them *Out for Justice*."

As recently as last week on Facebook, a friend posted a photo of the DVD, which he'd blind bought at a secondhand store, and wrote: "I'm led to believe that this is the GOOD Seagal movie right?"

To which I replied:

<u>Scott Bradley</u> It's not so much good but it's nuts and pretentiously begins with a quote from Arthur Miller.

That *Out for Justice* somehow acquired a degree of respectability and even acclaim in film buff circles has, I think, less to do with the movie itself and more what, on paper, the movie seems like it *could* have been.

The film originally had the more poetic title *The Price of Our Blood*, which was kiboshed by Warner Brothers; the studio wanted a three-word title along the lines of *Above the Law*, *Hard to Kill*, and *Marked for Death*.

The plot is simple and severe: Crackhead fuckup and "wannabe wiseguy" Richie Madano (a wonderfully snarling over-the-top performance by the great William Forsythe) kills cop Bobby Lupo (Joe Spataro) in broad daylight in front of the Bobby's family. It's the beginning of a day long crime spree with Richie running all over Brooklyn with his crew, killing people and generally fucking shit up. A third act "twist" reveals that Bobby was a crooked cop who was banging Richie's girlfriend (who

Richie snuffed before the movie begins) but that elicits little more than a shrug. The film would have been so much better if Richie had been a force of nature, a pure unrestrained Id monster with no motive like Alex in *A Clockwork Orange*, Patrick Bateman in *American Psycho*, or the Joker in *The Dark Knight*.

So Seagal is Gino Felino, NYPD cop. Bobby was his partner. And he and Bobby grew up with Richie in Brooklyn. That's where the Arthur Miller quote that opens the film comes in:

> "While to the stranger's eye one street was no different from another, we all knew where our 'neighborhood' somehow ended. Beyond that, a person was…a stranger."

Arthur Miller (1915-2005) was one of America's greatest playwrights, the Pulitzer Prize-winning legend who wrote *Death of a Salesman* and *The Crucible*. The quote in question is pulled from his essay "A Boy Grew in Brooklyn."

The ellipsis in *Out for Justice* is interesting. Here's the unedited quote: "It was a village, and while to the stranger's eye one street was no different from another, we all knew where our 'neighborhood' somehow ended, and the line of demarcation was never more than three blocks away. Beyond that, a person was somehow a stranger."

Part of me worries that the quote was edited because the word "demarcation" was deemed too difficult for the film's presumed audience.

I have always wondered if Arthur Miller knew about this film. He knew the movie industry well; he was married to Marilyn Monroe and wrote *The Misfits* (directed by John Huston) and the criminally underrated *Everybody Wins* (directed by Karel Reisz). His daughter Rebecca Miller is a filmmaker and married to Daniel Day-Lewis. Surely someone told him that a low-rent Steven Seagal actioner had quoted him? I would like to think so.

So, whose idea was the quote? Was it director John Flynn? He had a not uninteresting career prior to this movie: he made 1973's *The Outfit*, starring Robert Duvall in an adaptation of one of Donald Westlake/Richard Stark's Parker crime novels. He also directed 1977's *Rolling Thunder* (a Tarantino favorite, co-written by Paul Schrader) and *Best Seller* (a wonderful thriller starring Brian Dennehy and James Woods, written by Larry Cohen).

Maybe it was screenwriter David Lee Henry, the pseudonym of Canadian thriller writer R. Lance Hill. His credits include the Charles Bronson actioner *The Evil That Men Do* (based on his novel) and the much beloved *Roadhouse* starring Patrick Swayze. Henry/Hill is also credited with Oliver Stone on Hal Ashby's last film *Eight Million Ways to Die*, starring Jeff Bridges and Roseanna Arquette (though Robert Towne wrote the version that was made). Anyway…

Early in the film Gino sees an asshole dump a puppy. He rescues the puppy. The plot ensues but the puppy prevails and is named "Carragio" (Italian for Courage). This, honestly, is where the film fails: It rescues Gino's family unit – his wife suddenly doesn't want a divorce, his kid is fine, and the dog-abuser is taken to task (complete with the pooch pissing in the animal abuser's face).

Previous to this, Gino was as single-minded as Richie and they were locked in a Folie à deux. What do we make of that?

Let's be honest. If Scorsese had made this movie, it would be very different and very cool. Especially if written by Schrader or Richard Price.

But it's fine.

–Scott Bradley

Under Siege (1992)

I would love to go to Steven Segal's house for dinner. Have him cook up some Navy specialties. I bet you he took cooking classes to prepare for his role in Under Siege. I'd double down and say he even learned to cook under water. One day we'll have to eat underwater. One day we'll need the energy of Segal to save us from ourselves. Our personal chefs will be robotic shamans and Steven Segal's character Chef Casey Ryback will be the prototype. He will be our personal chef and body guard. We will have no natural enemies until the aliens come down because they're infinitely jealous of our singularity Steven Segal Chef Casey Ryback technology. They will beam down to capture and copy the tech, but these aliens will soon realize they made a drastic mistake when they face a battle to the death against your personal singularity bot Chef Casey Ryback. It will be like *Under Siege 3* but with aliens. This will be a masterpiece that God himself would watch. But Steven Segal is a Buddhist and his films and their possibilities are spiritual and psychological reflections of what it means to be human. It is not a mistake that the screenwriter created a character who is a master chef and *also* a master killer. The moment we killed our predators and lit fire to celebrate and nurture our survival we evolved into chefs and killers. The soul of man is in the food he eats and who he kills. Steven Segal is the chef who can kill and Steven Segal the Navy Seal can cook. Is this evidently the truth of a Yin & Yang? Or do we need to classify actions to a point where mysticism evaporates into the rain we drink or fight? Are we the captains of nuclear arsenal ships or are we the chefs that must cook and kill to keep the world from becoming radioactive?

Steven Segal is all and nothing. He is a man that neither accepts nor rejects modernity. He is at one with the fate of time. He is the shark that learned to walk and strike down the sun that beams with indifference. He is the measure of human progress that is adding and subtracting one hand clapping. Even though his captain died, he will command the ship. And by Captain, isn't God the captain who abandoned the ship or who was never there at all? Will the machines run the ships or will a Zen master run the machines? Was Under Siege more than a movie? Yes. Was it a mediation? Yes. Was it a message from the future? Was it to warn us that Gary Busey would one day challenge our understanding of sanity? Yes, but it was more than a yes and more than a no. It was a word that wasn't and won't be invented until we surpass what it means to live on the land and in the sea. There will be an *Under Siege 4*. It will be in space.

Only Steven Segal can handle life and death on and off Earth. Only Casey Ryback can learn how to kill and cook on other planets. Only only only is the song of Steven Segal. Only only only will be the song Steven Segal will sing into the space calling to the Tao of the Universe that will stop strangling itself into existence. And for a moment time space and matter will all look into Segal's eyes and say: I understand. The universe will enter Steven Segal and it will look to see itself not in a mirror but in action and it will travel back to 1992 to see itself on a screen with Segal cooking for the navy until Gary Busey and Tommy Lee Jones lock him up in the meat locker. The universe is a meat locker. It's a cold desolate world and the planets are meats on the hooks being cooked by the sun. But if the universe became at one with Steven Segal's Casey Ryback, it could know itself and therefore save itself. The ills of the future, like climate change, disease, and overpopulation, will have a showdown with Segal. Casey Ryback, the Zen singularity Gnostic Prophet will look into the eyes of the Demiurge. His stare will make the false gods fall into the oceans. The seas will devour the soul of silent devils and Casey Ryback will come down from Mars like Dr. Manhattan and cleanse the world of its fake-winged adversaries. Revelations is really just *Under Siege 5* and man will know peace and Gnostic Truth. But can man live with truth and peace and find purpose? No. Only if that man is Casey Ryback, but maybe he can teach us the way. Maybe he can show us a way where we are no longer chefs or hunters, but a ship at one with the waves and a train traveling to oneself—where the idea of land or sea are no longer there, and violence and peace become words with no meaning. We are only living in a world that Singularity Chef Bodyguard Casey Ryback sees and knows. We become one with his vision and a world of algorithms are assuaged into the angels we have become. The world is now dead and we all star in a new franchise, *Over Siege*, where we remake heaven, but god is not God but Casey Ryback, and the clouds are just his ship that he is steering for eternity. Where the devils like Tommy Lee Jones Boomer Band terrorists will fall into pits of the oceans, we could not save but our singularity selves will not need water or food. We will live a life without cooking or killing. We will become the siege that our souls needed to be at one with existence and the credits will roll and we will know true Zen in Casey Ryback's heaven. We will have become Casey Ryback. We are what we will be.

–Christoph Paul

Steven Seagal is... The Final Option (1993)

Admit it, you've always secretly fantasized about being Steven Seagal. I mean, who hasn't?

The money. The fame. The raw power of mastering aikido to the point where strangers' wrists spontaneously snap in your very presence. The feeling of an impeccably groomed ponytail cleaving the wind and slapping the sides of your neck as you run in that, um, "unique" way that you do. The philanthropic satisfaction of benefiting mankind forever by helping to make Erika Eleniak's topless scene in *Under Siege* a reality. And the transcendent sense of Buddhist Zen that comes from knowing that you don't even have to *try* to act to stay employed, so you don't.

What if I told you there was a way to finally experience what it's like walking a mile in Seagal's bulletproof kimono? Well, there is!

Kind of.

In 1993, California-based software publisher TecMagik announced the most exciting innovation in video games since the invention of the Power Glove. They would be releasing the first ever Steven Seagal video game for the Super Nintendo.

Before this, Seagal had been a lot of things. First, Steven Seagal was: *Above the Law*. Then, Steven Seagal was: *Hard to Kill*. After that, Steven Seagal was: *Marked for Death*. Next up, Steven Seagal was: *Out for Justice*. And last but not least, Steven Seagal was: *Under Siege* (along with Erika Eleniak and her considerable, ahem, "talents").

Now, *Steven Seagal is... The Final Option*.

Yes, that whole thing is the title, not just the last part. At least according to the start-up screen featured in the playable prototype.

See, *The Final Option* was never actually released. In an injustice matched only by the Academy of Motion Picture Arts and Sciences' failure to nominate Erika Eleniak's breasts in *Under Siege* for a Best Visual Effects Oscar, Seagal's one and only video game missed its planned 1994 release date. Then it missed its 1995 one. Then TecMagik announced that they would be retooling the game from the ground up under a new title, *The Deadly Hour,* in order to release it on the upcoming Nintendo 64 and Playstation consoles. Then TecMagik went out of business. Whoops!

But just like my penis when I see Erika Eleniak naked in *Under Siege,* you can't keep a good game down. That really has nothing to do with *The Final Option,* but it turns out you can't keep a *bad* game down either. In the early 2000s, an unfinished build of the game was finally leaked online, allowing anyone with an Internet connection and an exceptional capacity for self-loathing to play it.

Guess who has two thumbs and a clinical depression diagnosis? That's right, yours truly!

The first noteworthy thing about *The Final Option* is that it's not based on any pre-established Seagal property. In fact, in the game's story Seagal isn't even playing a character. He's playing himself! Not that it matters, as the plot is indecipherable—early reports summarized *The Final Option* as Seagal trying to woman's kidnapped son, while in-game files refer to the action star as a *Blade Runner*-esque future-cop fighting against an evil corporation called Nanotech.

Since Seagal is playing himself here, I can only assume that both of these potential plots are based on events that actually occurred in the actor's life.

Then again, what if it's not really Seagal at all?

That question brings us to the second noteworthy thing about *The Final Option*: its art style. Which is to say, it doesn't really have any "style." Its generic design combines hand-drawn sprites with digitized actors, à la *Mortal Kombat*. But in taking this approach, TecMagik accidentally painted themselves into a corner. They'd purchased the rights to Seagal's name, but they didn't actually negotiate Seagal's involvement.

Paying the then-popular Hollywood star's fee just to come in and throw a few karate chops in front of a green screen would've resulted in the game probably needing to retail for about $500 per unit—although its actual planned price of $70 isn't any less unconscionable. So TecMagik did the same thing the Mortal Kombat folks did when they couldn't get Jean-Claude Van Damme. They got someone who kinda-sorta-but-not-really looked like him.

Put some nobody's hair in a ponytail, slap a black leather jacket on him, and tell him to exert precisely zero effort. Voila, just as good as the real Seagal! And, most importantly, a *lot* cheaper.

To recap, we have a Steven Seagal game not based on any actual Steven Seagal property except for Steven Seagal himself, which Steven Seagal isn't even in because he's played by somebody else. Also, it takes place in the future. Maybe.

So how does it play?

Meh.

The Final Option is a fairly standard keep-walking-to-the-left-and-hitting-people game with some rudimentary platform elements. The main combat mechanics, aside from repeatedly tapping the punch and kick buttons, include throwing knives at enemies and shooting them with a handgun. There's also a combo that allows you to perform one of Seagal's patented low-energy aikido throws. Too often, though, players are tasked with jumping over pits of fiery lava or lime-green toxic waste. And just like the real Seagal, video game Seagal is not in any shape to be making leaps like that.

Fortunately, there are only six levels, and even though none of them are technically beatable due to the game's unfinished state, there is a mission select screen, meaning you can bounce around and see everything the game has to offer until you inevitably become bored and decide to do something better with your time. Like watch Erika Eleniak's *Under Siege* nude scene on a constant loop.

Simply put, if you're looking for entertainment *The Final Option* should be treated just like its title implies, as a last resort. Don't make it your Plan B. Don't even make it your Plan C, D, or E. This is strictly Plan Z material.

Not unlike watching one of Seagal's latter-day film efforts, *The Final Option* is an exercise in confusion and frustration. Unlike those movies, however, at least this video game's biggest failings can plausibly be chalked up to it never actually being completed, let alone released. Conversely, what the hell is *Under Siege 2*'s excuse?

I mean, that movie didn't even have Erika Eleniak in it. What a bust!

–William Tea

On Deadly Ground (1994)

On Deadly Ground (or, *How Steven Seagal Saved the Environment*) is quite possibly the most unapologetic Steven Seagal film ever made. It is not merely a Seagal vehicle, it is a Seagal film; produced and directed by Steven Seagal, starring Steven Seagal. This means that at the end of the day there wasn't anyone to tell him no. About anything. And what ensues is an hour and forty five minutes of Seagal thinking he has a socially conscious statement that is so mired in his own ego that any message is not only lost, but seems to make no sense.

Our film opens on an image of an eagle and begins a series of images of the majestic nature of Alaska. This pads the run time of the film, as it appears Seagal is attempting to say things with his camera that never really make an impact but seem an exercise in superfluous. And then the sound of a helicopter. We are about to be introduced to our hero of the film, Forrest Taft. And boy does he make an entrance. With flaming oil rig out of control, Taft (Seagal) steps from the helicopter wearing what seems to be an intentionally Native American styled jacket, dripping with fringe, he takes it off dramatically, lights a cigar with oil everywhere, and puts on a jumpsuit. He then struts to the fire, surveys the situation (he has already put out his cigar), and proceeds to create an explosion to stop the fire, so that now we just have oil pumping and spewing. His jumpsuit is clean, and he has saved the day through explosion. We're just getting started!

It is in this opening scene that we are also introduced to our one-dimensional, mustache-twirling villains played by Michael Caine and John C. McGinley. Caine is the head of our evil oil corporation and McGinley is his fixer/lackey whose go-to method of "fixing" things is through violence. There is no nuance to these characters at all, they serve to push the plot and the environmental message of our first-time director.

Caine has leased the oil rights from the local native tribe, and now has a tight deadline to get his oil rig online, or he has to give the rights back to the Natives. We are told through a whistle blower that what is causing the explosions is "bad preventers." This is never explained other than for the viewer to know that our evil corporation is purposely using faulty equipment to get their rig online before the deadline. When this info is discovered, people die!

However, when Forrest Taft is left for dead, he is rescued by those same natives that Big Oil is trying to swindle. When he wakes from near death and nearly steals a pack of sled dogs, it is clear that he is some kind of chosen one intended to go on a spiritual journey. The narcissism is so thick, it is mind boggling. Of course, only a spiritual white man in a ponytail, who whispers riddles can save the tribe and the environment. His forehead is touched by a feather, and he passes out into a state of spiritual journey. He not only wrestles a bear in slow motion, but also enters a cabin where he must make a choice between a chained, naked Native American woman and an older Native woman. He chooses the older woman, which seems to be the right choice, and gains some kind of knowledge. When he awakes, he is ready to fight Big Oil!

As he returns to civilization to fight our one-dimensional villains, he is accompanied by Joan Chen playing a Native American. Together they take on a band of mercenaries that include R. Lee Ermey and Billy Bob Thornton. Conveniently, there are huge caches of weapons in every cabin they end up in, and together they are able to fight off the evil henchman from one scene to the next. You better believe that it isn't only the bear that gets the respect of slow motion, but so many thugs going through windows or getting stabbed in the face very slowly! No one can accuse this film of lacking action, as there is much more of it than there is plot. That is what actually bogs this film down is its own complex about what it is. Is it an action movie with something to say? How much can it say about environmental responsibility if they blow up a helicopter in the beautiful Alaskan landscape?

Not only is this film hard to watch, but it seems as though one's brain cells are marked for death as they are constantly under siege by a string of contradictions. At the start of the film, Forrest asks an oil worker who has picked on a Native man, "What does it take to change the essence of a man?" This sentence echos throughout the film, partly because it seems to want to be a contemplative question that shows us the introspective nature of our hero. Instead, it is whispered in a manner that one can almost hear Seagal improving this line as he knows the importance it will serve in the film. It doesn't, but it is very telling of the film Seagal thinks he's delivering, and so it is when Forrest Taft makes his final move on the oil rig to stop them from getting it online, he blows it up! He blows up an oil rig in order to save the environment! There is some sort of line about preventing the spill, yet there is oil everywhere. Every single villain dies in some sort of oily ending, and the entirety of its social commentary seems confused by its action!

In the end, Seagal delivers a speech about saving the environment, about being responsible for life on this planet. As he does so, images of oil-covered animals plays visually. Again, there is an effort to be serious, and deliver a message. It does reflect the deaths of the films villains covered in oil, but the viewer is left wondering what it is that just happened. How did this film attract the talents of Michael Caine? Who thought allowing Seagal to direct was a good idea? Why on Earth would anyone blow up an oil rig to save the environment? But that's what happens when you're living on deadly ground!

–Chris Brown

Under Siege 2: Dark Territory (1995)

Dark Territory is named for the area of the train track where conductors can't converse with one another, which is how the train ends up on a collision course with another train. That definition actually gives the sequel an intelligent meaning and makes it one of the most intelligent movie titles Seagal has done.

Seagal is back as Casey Ryback, the heroic chef from the hit film *Under Siege*. This time he takes care of his niece after his brother dies in a plane crash. One the way to its destination the train gets hijacked by terrorist Travis Dane, played wonderfully by Eric Bogosian. Travis worked on a satellite to help destroy underground targets, he was later fired for his mental instability, a trait that seems to have fallen by the wayside since Travis, while being an evil murderer, does seem to know what he is doing and has complete control of his mental functions. The terrorist group take the hostages into the last two cars of the train and that's when Ryback does what he does best, he makes a delicious three course meal, just kidding, he starts to drop body after body.

Ryback eventually teams up with a porter, played by Morris Chestnut. Together they try to stop the terrorists from blowing up a generator located underneath the pentagon. Morris Chestnut would actually not learn his lesson at all, as he would go on to play a villain in the movie *Half Past Dead*, this time going against Seagal, which really shows that Chestnut was determined to become the master.

Katherine Heigel, in one of her earliest performances, plays Sarah, who just seems to function as a hostage Dark to give Ryback a sense of why he is doing what he is doing. She has bit at the end, of course after she becomes the obligatory damsel in distress. It almost becomes cliche as to what to do with this character, could the movie have functioned without her, I mean he could visit his brother's funeral, just because it's his brother.

Now that we have shown that there is a little intelligence in making *Dark Territory* work, let's focus on the absurdity of the movie. The people at the pentagon already know Ryback from his help with the submarine situation from Under Siege, so they are a little more confident and generally surprised to see him on this train. I feel there is an insert shot of a General going, "Casey Ryback is on this train?" just so the suspension of disbelief is not as severe. Is it still severe if there is a character who doesn't believe it as much as the audience? Also with train movies, what is the plan? You can see where the train is going, just attack it, but whatever, we would have a shorter movie if we did that, I know. Also, when the inevitable head on collision with another train happens, you see Ryback give the middle finger to physics and run to the end of the train to beat the crash, which means he pretty much just teleports to the end of the train.

The character development could have been so much more. Yes, we all see the disgruntled employee, who gets fired for having mental health issues, this is actually a joke in the first movie with Gary Busey dressed as a woman asking Tommy Lee Jones if he looks like he has mental health issues and Tommy going deadpan saying, "Not at all." They also have several call backs to the original. Ryback hides in a freezer in the beginning, he is forced to deal with a reluctant side kick. In the first, it was Miss July, a stripper jumping out of a cake, which is probably one fo the greatest entrances for a side kick ever put on film. What this one does with the side kick is amazing, the first one had her reluctant, this one, the porter wants to kick some ass and take names, including a scene of Ryback showing the porter a martial arts move, which if you have seen any action movie where the master teaches a move to someone, that move will come back later on, and it does.

Eric Bogosian chews the scenery as Travis Dane. You could tell he had a lot of fun playing this role. His chief underling also has his moment to shine when he is pepper sprayed and he explains that he has been pepper sprayed so many times, he almost seems to enjoy it.

This one had critics on its side as well, it is a wonderful companion piece to the first one. It has enough call backs to the first to make the audience smile, without feeling like they paid money to see the same movie twice. Is it absurd? Of course, what Seagal movie isn't?

The audience had a blast. It opened to #2 at the box office, behind *Apollo 13*. It also grossed over 100 million dollars. There was talk about doing a third *Under Siege* movie, however those talks seemed to have ended. There has also been talks of mistreatment by Seagal to Katherine Heigel, disgusted when he told her that he has girlfriends her age (she was 16 at the time). There was also an alleged incident where Seagal tried to get Jenny McCarthy to do a nude scene that wouldn't be filmed.

Dark Territory will always have to live in the shadow of its predecessor, which isn't a bad   thing. It gave the audience a thrill and excellent counter programming to the family friendly *Apollo 13*. It makes one wonder what Seagal has in mind if he ever wants to do a third movie. What mode of transportation will he be on? How will he hide in a freezer, who will his reluctant side kick be? What mental illness will the main protagonist have? Is there a checklist that he follows to make sure it's classified as an *Under Siege* movie?

–Stephen Kessen

Executive Decision (1996)

Faced with the task of looking back on the career of Steven Seagal, it was easy to choose *Executive Decision,* as it's the best movie he has appeared in. *Under Siege* is certainly the high-water mark of Seagal's career. But that's a movie *starring* Seagal. Another advantage of *Executive Decision* is the filmmaker's choice to kill off Seagal at the climax of the first act, 45 minutes into the picture. I have to believe the creative team of this movie saw his previous work and recognized the best thing Steven Seagal can do in your movie is put his name on the poster, then die horribly.

Executive Decision is the kind of middling mid-90s actioner that has played on late-night cable for decades. It isn't even the first (or the best) "*Die Hard* on a Plane" movie. And the story of generic bad guy Islamic fundamentalists, led by David Suchet with a suspect tan, is thinly contrived to move us from one suspenseful beat to another every twenty minutes or so. There's not a lot of character to these characters. It cribs from every other trendy trope of its time; why not steal a fun idea from *Psycho?*

Seagal, as Lieutenant Colonel Austin Travis, seems to be here just to get main character Dr. Jack Ryan David Grant (Kurt Russell), onto the hijacked plane. Travis leads a crack commando team, and in his limited screen time we see the zeitgeist of a Seagal performance. He kills eight people in three minutes – the first three after he comes out of the trees with a knife – slitting throats and backstabbing. I've watched it twice and I'm still not sure if he has any lines.

But Seagal cares about more than just violence. Most of his roles carry at least an undercurrent of camaraderie and revenge. Someone close to him dies – now he's motivated to get the bad guys and avenge his dead friend or coworker. In *Executive Decision,* that's a member of his commando squad who is taken by surprise moments before the team realizes the nerve gas is long gone and the whole mission is a bust.

We don't see Travis for another fifteen minutes after that raid, as the movie sets up the terrorist hijacking and kills off Mary Ellen Trainor (in between *Lethal Weapons 3* and *4*). But we have to imagine in the three months since that fateful day he has longed to stick it to somebody, anybody, for wasting his time and getting his man killed. Travis blames Grant, an army intelligence expert, for the entire ill-conceived mission. So, he decides to bring Grant with him on the next dangerous mission, in an untested spy plane, presumably just to give him a scare. We don't know if they have any other shared history. They barely exchange words.

"This is the prick who sent us on a wild goose chase," whispered to one of the other Army guys, is one of Seagal's longest sentences and his only clear motivation. Really, it's the only character moment that adds anything to our understanding of Austin Travis. He "wrote the book on assaulting hijacked aircraft," and he gives Grant a withering death stare once he has dragged him along for the ride.

Between that and his heroic sacrifice shortly thereafter, we don't get to know Travis. Oddly, he seems to genuinely want Grant's advice over the radio during the upcoming operation that Travis won't live to see. But his death, and the loss of the spy plane, is caused entirely by his dramatic need to be in charge. He arbitrarily gives civilian contractor Oliver Platt orders to get on the 747 first, despite good reasons to the contrary. He's inflexible, and impatient.

Shortly before his big death scene, Travis confronts Grant about the nerve gas mission, and states plainly the thematic point of Lt. Col. Austin Travis: on a mission he doesn't believe in, with the reluctant Dr. Grant ("Who the hell else is going to do it? You?") in tow. Almost immediately, Seagal flails as the daring plane-to-plane commando transfer falls apart and everyone else makes it out alive.

That's why it's important to remember this is a movie *with* Steven Seagal, not a Steven Seagal movie. He's barely there. And once he gets out of the way, there's time for Halle Berry to show us why she's going to become a big star. And for John Leguizamo, B.D. Wong, and Joe Morton to do all the tough guy stuff. It's an action movie that is smart enough to sideline one conventional action hero to give everybody else a chance to band together and get the job done. There's something weird and wonderful about B.D. Wong sporting a flattop and putting on a Southern accent while chewing gum on his way to kick ass.

Frankly, Seagal is outclassed by Russell in every scene. Even when positioned as a bookish research guy, I can't not see Snake Plissken sitting there waiting to take over the movie. Some years later Leguizamo appeared on *Late Night with Conan O'Brien* and recalled how Seagal argued on the set of *Executive Decision* that Travis shouldn't die.

"I can hold the planes together like this," Leguizamo demonstrated, striking a wild Superman pose imitating Seagal reaching out to hold two supersonic planes together.

The powers that be told Seagal he was an idiot and proceeded as scripted, thus giving us what I consider his best movie. The one where a miniature Seagal is visibly blown out into the sky at 30,000 feet without a parachute. Die hard, indeed.

–Michael Rizzo

The Glimmer Man (1996)

Welcome to *The Glimmer Man,* a 1996 buddy cop movie starring Steven Seagal and Keenan Ivory Wayans. The opening credits ensure we know this movie was made in the 90s by using blurry side-scrolling views of an urban street, with quick cut plot points interspersed with the credits that all have the "negative film" effect applied.

Fresh off his breakout portrayal as the Mailman (MESSAGE!) in *Don't Be A Menace to South Central While Drinking Your Juice in the Hood* we see Detective Jim Campbell (Wayans) rushing through a police bullpen. He arrives at his office to find our hero, Jack Cole (Seagal), sitting at his desk dressed all in black, with prayer beads around his neck. Campbell is already angry with Cole for sitting at his desk, until Cole reveals he has been assigned to the "Family Man" case. A fresh set of victims gives us a quick rundown on the modus operandi of the killer (crucified victims) as the latest victims are inspected. Supercop Cole tells everyone that these victims aren't the same as the others, something only he can see as the rest of the 20 detectives are convinced this is the same.

We cut to a partner bonding moment in the car back to the station when Cole accepts a call for a suicide at a nearby school. We arrive at the Catholic school (yes, the Catholic undertones are strong throughout) to find that it isn't a suicide as much as it is a hostage situation. When Cole finds out the student holding the hostages has been in therapy, he is sure to make a joke about the kid having the wrong therapist. Cole then goes on to use two cell phones and the school P.A. system to lure the student, Johnny, holding the hostages to the window so he can enter the room, and then tackle Johnny through the window, across a gap, and into the art room. After the events, Cole is thanked profusely by Johnny's stepdad for only breaking a few of his stepson's ribs as opposed to shooting him. There may have well been a giant sign saying "Bad Guy." We hit the morgue for some witty banter about the victim's tits and more Supercop power demonstrations of Cole identifying the victim's nationality by sight alone and mutilating a corpse to remove a breast implant.

An inexplicable scene in a Chinese pharmacy brings racial stereotypes into the mix. First Campbell indicates that because he's black, there is no way he could speak Chinese. Then Cole doses Campbell with an allergy medicine; powdered deer penis. I can only think this scene happens to set up a "suck on some deer penis" joke later in the movie.

We have reached the 20-minute mark in the movie and have yet to see Mr. Seagal show off those trademark lightning-fast hands, so obviously we need a scene where Cole and Campbell are outnumbered 3 to 1. Cole takes out eight of the guys, three with just a trick credit card that hides a razor, and Campbell struggles to take out the one.

Another set of victims is found, but this time Cole is uncharacteristically quiet, relying solely on Seagal's "sour face" acting to show something is amiss. We find that one of the victims is his ex-wife and Cole goes home to tell his kids their mother is dead while Campbell gets suspicious, more so when Cole's fingerprint is found on his ex-wife's body. Welcome to *The Glimmer Man* act 2, this time it's personal.

While the viewer learns that Cole was a CIA operative, Campbell is using the limited resources of the LAPD intelligence department to investigate Cole's past. After nothing is found other than Cole's time in the NYPD, Campbell decides to confront Cole AT HIS EX WIFE'S FUNERAL! Cole is pissed so he heads to a restaurant to see his old boss from the CIA. The host gets a bit mouthy, so Cole knocks him out by slapping him across the face. Obviously, this restaurant gets destroyed just because it's been another 10 minutes and Seagal hasn't had to hit someone. A random art teacher identifies the "Family Man" killer, causing Cole to head to a church to confront and kill the suspect on his own inside a church. He then, as an apparent sign of remorse, holds the gun he just fired by the barrel with both hands. This gets him drummed off the force.

Wait, you thought we were done? Nope. That wasn't even the first boss. We see the REAL bad guys meeting to figure out what loose ends to tie up. One of the bad guys being… Cole's old CIA boss, the other Johnny's Stepdad! The bad guys use a combination of hitmen and explosions while cleaning up their loose ends, with no success. It is exceptionally hard to kill guys that can outrun gas explosions after all. Our heroes reunite in a theater where Campbell is crying to *Casablanca*, they then head off to save Johnny from the CIA. The partners use a series of phone calls and tape recordings to turn the bad guys against each other and get them to mostly kill each other, and obviously clear Cole in the process. Of course, one must escape to they can have a one on one showdown with Cole so Steven Seagal can show off those sweet, sweet martial arts moves.

As cliché and stereotypical this movie is, I still find enjoyment in it. It is like a B-horror flick, the worse it is the more enjoyable. This is pretty standard Steven Seagal fare, not nearly as many fights as other movies, but we get plenty of him standing with his hands clasped together and more than a few "emotional" moments where Steven can show off his "I just ate a whole lemon" face, not to mention his parade of garish jackets that would make Joe Exotic jealous.

–Pat Kawula

Roseanne (1996)

Things are crazy. I am writing in the United States in 2020, a year defined by political clashes, protests about racial injustice, waves of economic uncertainty and inequality, and a global pandemic. Regardless of your ideological views, things are far from normal. Given that lack of normalcy, I would like to discuss Roseanne Barr and Steven Seagal.

Early in their careers, both Barr and Seagal earned praise for their commitments to "progressive issues" in their respective entertainments: Roseanne Barr's television coverage of working-class struggles and Steven Seagal's cinematic focus on environmentalism. Many early Seagal movies provide leftist critiques of government, and in 2012 Barr lost the Green Party presidential nomination to Jill Stein. Seagal and Barr used to occupy liberal positions on political issues. More recently, both celebrities have skewed to far-right conservativism, embracing right-wing conspiracy theories. Steven Seagal now serves as Russia's goodwill ambassador to the U.S. at Vladimir Putin's request, and Seagal has delivered live interviews in front of the Kremlin criticizing American citizens for protesting racial inequality. Roseanne Barr has become an avid Trump supporter and made her "Roseanne" character in the show's revival just as enthusiastically right-wing, and Barr has provocatively dressed up in a swastika armband and Hitler costume for a photo shoot with *Heeb*, pulling burnt gingerbread people out of an oven. While these summaries of celebrity political views remove aspects of context, these bizarre choices almost defy context and explanation.

And yet the two celebrities share the context of appearing in a *Roseanne* episode called "Roseambo," where Barr's titular character defeats a gang of terrorists while riding with her family on a train. The terrorists' depictions—white, black, and Asian, featuring fake beards and a spectrum of dissonant ethnic signifiers in clothes and accents—provide some of the episode's campy humor, along with Roseanne's wholly unconvincing fight choreography. After defeating the would-be hijackers, Roseanne is visited by "Hillary Clinton" and Steven Seagal, who literally appears and disappears like a ghost at the end of the episode, whispering a few words about the Buddhist search for nothingness. The episode's best gag features Roseanne blowing a tampon out of its tube like a deadly poison dart into a terrorist's eye as Roseanne delivers a cocky action one-liner: "Now you can ride horses and swim." It's a damn weird episode.

Roseanne aired its first episode in 1988, the same year as Steven Seagal's acting debut in *Above the Law*. The sitcom famously depicted a dysfunctional, loving family struggling to survive poverty and hardship, but the social commentary was undermined when Roseanne won the lottery in the show's ninth season. Episodes were nonsensical and self-indulgent: Dan's mother tries to kill him (which the show effectively did at the end of the season) or Roseanne's sister dates a prince. The ninth season is a bizarre mishmash, much like its opening credits with their uncanny computerized morphing of the cast members' faces, and "Roseambo" is part of that weirdly shapeshifting insanity.

After the stiff, unrealistic fight scenes and corny jokes, Steven Seagal materializes to congratulate Roseanne, his "grasshopper." Roseanne claims she studied the master's teachings, "especially those available on video." Seagal chastises her for using violence, saying: "you need to realize that the only enemy is within you. If you can dissolve into emptiness, you'll realize that you cannot resist that which doesn't exist. This is the true nature of shunyata." He then literally dissolves into emptiness, leaving just how he arrived.

Seagal advises Roseanne to embrace nothingness, a fitting thesis to an episode of tepid action movie parody in a sitcom that ultimately decides to "undo" everything by revealing that Roseanne never won the lottery and instead fantasized the season's episodes to cope with her husband's death. In other words, nothing matters. The reveal that Dan died in season eight renders the substance of season nine meaningless, yet the ending achieves poignancy by depicting Roseanne as a grieving widow who finds solace and her identity through writing. But the 2018 revival of *Roseanne* reverses Dan's death with a lame joke that renders even those final moments meaningless.

Perhaps this meaninglessness is the whole point. If the only enemy is within you, if dissolving into emptiness is truly the goal of figures like Steven Seagal and his "grasshopper" Roseanne Barr, then their public statements of personal beliefs are not contradictory. While their views might have veered somewhat chaotically to the right, perhaps these changes are not hypocrisy but a soul-deep commitment to the only constant being change. Such contradictions might be a kind of performative Zen Buddhist koan as enacted by Seagal and Barr, paralleling Roseanne's 1997 meditation in what she believed was the series finale prior to *Roseanne*'s 2018 revival: "I was so angry I was more like a female Steven Seagal wanting to fight the whole world." As her master claims, the whole world is not the enemy; the enemy is within.

Of course, the self-annihilation inherent in the semi-mystical words of Steven Seagal's cameo in a dopey episode of *Roseanne* eventually became literalized for Barr. When *Roseanne* was revived, the characters dismissed Dan's death (and most of the final season's non-canonical absurdity) with a joke, undoing it. Then, in May 2018, after Barr tweeted a racially charged attack against one of Obama's senior advisors, ABC canceled the show, the incident being a conservative controversy from Roseanne Barr that went too far for them to overlook. And so the show killed off Roseanne herself, rebranding as a spinoff called *The Conners*, making the sitcom a kind of meta-fictional Frankenstein's monster capable of destroying its own creator. I do not know if this swift reaction on ABC's part is social media justice—or if Steven Seagal's self-exile from Hollywood aims at a similar vein of self-destructive behavior comparable to Barr's—but it does speak to the wisdom in "Roseambo" that Steven Seagal speaks and Roseanne Barr seems to endorse: that they are both their own worst enemies.

–Greg Wright

Fire Down Below (1997)

EPA agent Jack Taggert is on a mission. Find out what's polluting a small town in Appalachia, and change leather jackets at least three times a day. Portly practitioner of Aikido Steven Seagal is back in the environmental thriller, *Fire Down Below.* The cast may be one of the most interesting parts of the film. Noted character actors Harry Dean Stanton and Stephen Lang have standout performances, as well as leading lady Marg Helgenberger. It's actually a bit puzzling how many talented people were involved in the project, especially considering its rigid protagonist.

Seagal stars as Jack Taggart, an oddly docile yet trigger happy sort that is...less than believable as a human being, much less a environmental protector. The martial arts luminary seems something like an alien in human disguise with his odd gait and wooden movements. As the opening credit montage exposits, several other agents have been sent to the tiny hamlet to investigate possible illegal waste dumping. It's truly hard to pick up most of these important plot points, as they're happening in disjointed flashbacks as loud music overlays. I can't help but wonder if these scenes originally were intended to be separate, but the director noticed the lack of his star's ability to seem interested in being in them and decided to edit it all together and hope for the best. But let's be frank, this is a Steven Seagal movie, we aren't here for the plot.

Taggart travels to the remote town of Jackson, Kentucky where he's met by the local pastor, played by Southern Rock drummer, Levon Helm. Helm has been the EPA's contact in the town and offers Seagal a small apartment beneath the church and a list of possible leads on the dumping. Using the cover of a handyman, doing God's work, he offers his services free of charge to any willing local yokels. I have to say, the interactions between these southern folk and Seagal are absolutely hilarious. It would seem we're supposed to get the idea that through these interactions,

Taggart is finding a love for the people and their plight. Unfortunately, Seagal seems at best uninterested and at worst flat out disgusted by them.

We meet the antagonists fairly quickly in the form of the local sheriff and a group of random hillbilly thugs working for villain's idiot son. The Sheriff gives Jack the old "You stay out of trouble boy!" speech and Seagal smirks his way through, oblivious or unafraid of the threats. Our title villain, Orin Hanner Sr., is played by singer/songwriter/actor and all around stone cold badass, Kris Kristofferson. Though his scenes in the movie are sparse, he chews up scenery like a woodchipper, showing a boyish charm and devil may care flair few others can combine. In writing this, it really strikes me how great the supporting cast performs. They really could have coasted through and collected the paycheck. Seagal himself certainly did. Fortunately for Taggart, the thugs are all completely inept and only attack him one at a time. Hanner Sr. is using his hometown to dump chemicals in an abandoned mining facility, which is poisoning the aquifer and endangering the town.

We can't have an action movie without a helpless love interest to rescue, and Marg Helgenberger's Sarah Kellog is your prototypical lost lady with a secret past. The town shuns her because she was implicated in a mysterious house fire that killed her father. She's looking for a hero and to sell her homemade honey to the less than interested locals. The chemistry between Taggart and Sarah is non-existent. After meeting her at the church picnic, he steals her heart by fixing her porch steps. Which he does in a heavy leather duster and black button up. I've had a lot of work on my house recently, but I've yet to see any workman in this particular get up. Segal's leather jackets almost deserve cast credit, as in a single day, he wears no less than three separate ones. The best of which, is a fringed tan suede number that has to be seen to be believed.

Through his, I guess you could call it research, Taggart is drawn to another local, a timid farmer that seems to know more than he lets on. Harry Dean Stanton plays Cotton Harry, a concerned citizen that secretly sent Taggart a letter about the dumping. He loves his home, but fears

Hanner's goons and is reluctant to offer help. After some more awkward mumblesations, he agrees to help. After offering assistance in finding the dumping grounds, Taggart takes water samples and talks about the aquifer in a hilariously awkward set of scenes. While Taggart is off 'romancing' Sarah, Cotton takes a severe beating by the hillbilly henchman and is left for dead. During said, "romancing" we meet the final oddly placed villain, Sarah's brother Earl. Earl is played with an "aw shucks" charm, with sinister undertones, by Stephen Lang. Lang truly shines as this glad-handing prick with a shit eating grin and all the class of a used car salesman. It turns out he has a disturbing sexual interest in his sister and doesn't like Taggart sniffing around his territory.

After Taggart finds Cotton broken and bleeding, he faces off with the Sheriff and his men, revealing himself as a federal agent and severely beats several deputies in a show of defiance. Several leather jacket changes later, he and Sarah attend the local fair and we get to see Steven Seagal: Bluegrass guitar picker. You heard me. This also translated to real life as Seagal formed a Bluegrass band and released several albums. No seriously, he really did. We finally get a one-on-one showdown with Kristoffersons' Hanner. This is a serious highpoint. The first actual chemistry Seagal shows with anyone is in this scene. These two really chew some serious scenery. From this point, we start building to the climax. Hanners men burn down the church, killing the pastor and Seagal vows revenge…again. We kick into overdrive as Earl heel turns on Taggart, trapping him in the mine with the chemicals and locking up Sarah so he can do unspeakable things to her later. Seagal is a one-man army, effortlessly taking down a passel of goons and blowing up the mine and chemicals in spectacular action movie fashion. This of course is a ruse, and she's kidnapped by a six-gun toting Randy Travis. But this is not enough for Jack Taggart. No, he has one final showdown with Hanner in the villain's casino, beating the living bejeesus out of his guards and shooting Hanner in the process. Hanner is arrested, tried and found guilty, sentenced to a paltry fine. Hanner thinks he's off scott free until Seagal returns with the FBI who arrest Hanner for attempted murder and various other charges.

The bad guy is behind bars and Taggart can finally live happily ever after with Sarah as the movie draws to a close. By the standards of Steven Seagal movies, this is by far one of the best. The supporting cast is excellent and seem determined to make this walking mannequin in a fringe cowboy duster look passable. *Fire Down Below* would go on to be a modest box office success, one of the last few Seagal movies not to go straight to DVD. The people of Appalachia are safe, and they have the ponytailed prince of punch and kick to thank. Is it high art? Is it impressive and memorable cinema? Fuck no. It is however a fun, engaging, well-made entry into the pantheon of Steven Seagal's mindless action catalog.

–Todd Davidson

The Patriot (1998)

During the early 1970s, William C. Heine, a journalist-turned-author, penned *The Last Canadian*, his first novel. Set in an apocalyptic North America, it concerns Eugene Arnprior, a Montreal engineer who finds himself on the run from a deadly plague. With his wife and children in tow, he races against time to reach a remote cabin in rural Canada. From one page to the next, the story remains spellbinding. Approximately twenty-five years following the publication of Heine's novel, the motion picture rights were acquired by Steven Seagal and producer Julius R. Nasso, but many modifications were sought. The setting, for example, abruptly changed to Montana. It was also decided Seagal's Sun Ranch, located near Yellowstone National Park, would provide a suitable filming location. Screenwriters M. Sussman and John Kingswell ultimately set their adaptation in Ennis, Montana, approximately thirty miles north of the ranch. Entitled *The Patriot*, principal photography of Seagal's film commenced in September of 1997.

Floyd Chisolm (Gailard Sartain), described by the press as a neo-Nazi with a history of radical confrontations, proudly refers to himself as the "patriot" of a new America. To prove a point and eradicate those who oppose his philosophy, he exposes the community to NAM-37, a lethal toxin. When an airborne virus starts claiming lives, Wesley McClaren (Seagal), a local doctor, takes it upon himself to find a solution. He and his young daughter, Holly (Camilla Belle), are mysteriously unaffected. Due to her immunity, she becomes a target of Chisolm's militia. They desperately seek a cure. Audiences come to learn Holly and McClaren have consumed a special tea containing wildflowers, which are the antidote. Chisolm, meanwhile, is featured as a secondary obstacle to the town's liberation, and in order to be established as a ruthless antagonist, he occasionally resorts to cold-blooded murder. It is therefore suggested audiences should be gratified when McClaren penetrates Chisolm's skull with, oddly enough, the broken stem of a wine glass. At such a point of the narrative, however, *The Patriot* has featured its share of mistakes and therefore cannot be taken seriously.

An example pertains to the supporting character of Frank (L.Q. Jones). He is presented to audiences as a respected friend of McClaren, but midway through the narrative, his unexpected theatrics are not only out of character for him, they also seal his fate. Earlier, Frank and Holly discuss U.S. states, particularly Mississippi. Without hesitation, she correctly spells it. Frank then asks if she can accomplish the same feat without the use of "eyes." Holly, believing he is referring to the vowel of "I," becomes stumped. Frank covers his eyes and amusingly spells Mississippi. Despite such a silly display of affection, it becomes clear he maintains a realistic, hard-nosed approach to life. Frank later confronts Dr. "Little Richard" Bach (Dan Beene), a colleague of McClaren's, at the hospital. Answers are demanded. "We're trained and equipped for this," Bach manages, but his uncertainty is apparent. The shrewd Frank presses the issue. He seeks a straight answer, one Bach is unable to provide. Frank is a man who refuses to be outwitted. At one point, he single-handedly dismantles Chisolm's henchmen, who have stormed the ranch in search of Holly. In the immediate aftermath of victory, however, the unexpected transpires. Contrary to Frank's personality, he suddenly becomes oblivious. His back is turned to the militia's lone survivor, who appears dead but is only wounded. McClaren, meanwhile, has witnessed the battle from afar and immediately progresses toward the area. As Frank faces his oncoming friend, he crows and performs a jig. Chisolm's surviving henchman seizes the opportunity to fire a single shot. Incidentally, the bullet rips through Frank's chest. When he earlier tricked Holly with the spelling riddle, he was being silly. To abruptly dance after a firefight, however, is an act of stupidity. Furthermore, after the bullet strikes its target, McClaren does not rush to his friend's side. He instead remains stationary and sulks as Frank lay dying.

Later, McClaren arrives at a secret, underground military installation. As he wanders its corridors, natural sunlight, protruding from several doorways, becomes visible. The scene was filmed not underground, but on the third floor of the Engineering and Physical Science Building of Montana State University. In spite of the film's flaws, director Dean Semler, to a limited degree, rights a wrong when presenting the memorable image of an Ennis billboard. The city is dubbed the fly-fishing capital, and its tagline, teasing passing motorists, ironically proclaims, "Hope you caught something!"

Principal photography of *The Patriot* concluded on November 11, 1997. It was released theatrically in Spain on July 10, 1998. Reviews were mostly negative. As a result, The Patriot did not garner much interest from domestic distributors. HBO finally agreed to purchase the film and broadcast it on February 6, 1999. The following month, Native American performer Leonard Mountain Chief, who appeared in the film as the enchanting Grandpa, died of a heart attack. His character is unquestionably the most vital of the narrative, because without him, there would be no wildflower tea to destroy the virus. Regarding the film's production, it transpired primarily without incident. On one occasion, the cast and crew were in Virginia City, Montana, to film an outdoor scene when snow began to fall. Most of the filming had already been completed. In addition, none of the other outdoor scenes featured snow.

Seagal and company therefore deemed it best to wait. The snow continued to fall for two days straight. Once it stopped, crews intervened. "We had to melt [the snow], sweep it, rake it, anything to get rid of it," location manager Mark Zetler said. As filming wrapped approximately two weeks later, he nevertheless declared "everything's worked out." Seagal decided he no longer had a use for Sun Ranch and sold it to tech entrepreneur Roger Lang a short time later, and when the local press inquired as to the star's future plans, he was rumored to be leaving for Nepal, where spiritual guidance and renewal from a Buddhist mentor would supposedly be sought.

–J. R. Jordan

Haines, Joan. "Seagal wraps up filming of 'The Patriot'." *Bozeman Daily Chronicle*. November 11, 1997. "Mining company CEO buys Sun Ranch near Yellowstone Park." *Associated Press*. February 2, 2010.

Exit Wounds (2001)

The final movie Mr. Flappy Hands made under Warner Bros, the studio that gave him his break with 1988's Andrew Davis helmed *Above the Law*, or *Nico* as it was known in some territories, *Exit Wounds* feels like a relic from its time only with a couple of script revisions in order for it to appeal to the kids.

The movie opens with a speech by the Vice President who is attacked by the Michigan Militia disguised as motorcycle cops. There's a certain amount of eye-rolling that you'll do throughout this film and this sequence is a prime example with the use of a cheap-looking helicopter model & an unconvincing dummy hit by Seagal, playing Orin Boyd in the delivery van he's using to help the VP escape. The opening is a rejected script idea from *Lethal Weapon 4* screenwriter Jeffrey Boam that was repurposed for this film and part of reshoots that pushed up the production budget by $8 million from its original $25 million.

It's due to this incident with Boyd, which ended with the Al Gore-like vice president being thrown into a Michigan river, explaining why he's transferred to the infamous 15th precinct for uniform duties and he meets a band of cops who may or may not be corrupted all under the command of Jill Hennessey a former member of Internal Affairs, forcing Boyd with the mysterious Latrell Walker, played actor/rapper DMX, to team up by the end of the film to take down bad guys.

The script, based on a book from former cop John Westermann and adapted by Ed Horowitz and Richard D'Ovidio, bares little to no resemblance to the source novel aside from the method the bad guys used to transport the heroin through vacuum packed T-shirts. There are references to the dot.com bubble of the late 90s that Latrell Walkers became rich during, Puff Daddy, and technology that ages the film terribly.

Exit Wounds was helmed by the polish-born cinematographer turned director Andrzej Bartkowiak who has credits working with the likes of Sidney Lumet and John Huston made this the middle movie in his Urban Trilogy which began with Shakespeare-inspired *Romeo Must Die* starring Jet Li and ending with the 2003 *Cradle to the Grave*, starring DMX and Li, which supposedly took ideas from Fritz Lang's *M*.

The fight sequences are over the top and choreographed by Dion Lam who has worked in both Hong Kong and Hollywood with his subsequent films being *The Matrix* sequels. Mr Lam's wirework isn't on the same level as *Crouching Tiger Hidden Dragon* but it does make the fight scenes stand out with one stellar shootout involving Latrell Walker that may have taken inspiration from *Tiger On The Beat* starring Chow Yun Fat and a sword fight that has the feel of HK action flick.

Exit Wounds' score by Jeff Rona and Damon "Grease" Blackman has music from Ja Rule, DMX & strangely, Moby's "Come On Baby," memorably used in the robbery sequence from 1995's *Heat* directed by Micheal Mann, to announce when Boyd meets Walker in this film.

If you though the comedic moments in *The Glimmer Man* involving Powdered Deer Penis were painful, then the scenes with Tom Arnold's morning tv show host Henry Wayne that Orin Boyd meets in an anger management class will resonate. This includes a sequence with Seagal's character conducting traffic badly to James Brown's "I Feel Good." This is a scene that wouldn't look out of place in the Jim Belushi canine "classic" *K9* even as it ended with Anthony Anderson and Tom Arnold in a cringeworthy improv battle.

At the time of this film's release it was seen as a comeback for Seagal after the less than stellar box office of the *Se7en* rip off, *The Glimmer Man*, and poor reception for *Fire Down Below* (which was one of the factors along with a string of other Warner Bros flops not to go beyond pre-production including the Tim Burton helmed *Superman Lives* starring Nicolas Cage as The Man of Steel), and 1998's *The Patriot* skipping theatres all together in his first movie for Sony.

It does have the sheen of a Joel Silver–produced film to the film's benefit. *Exit Wounds* would be Seagal's biggest box office opening, taking $19 million domestically and ending up with a worldwide gross of $79 million with critics giving it a mixed reception. Speaking of, Jonathan Foreman in his New York Post review suggests that Andrzej Bartkowiak was trying to make a John Woo movie but didn't have the talent to do so. For me, though? *Exit Wounds* is Seagal's Dirty Harry when it comes to the rest of his acting career.

–Aaron Carruthers

Ticker (2001)

There are important things to know about *Ticker*, but they need context. For instance, the list of Steven Seagal movies that I remember watching ends right before this one, which I hadn't even heard of. Having now seen it, I understand why.

Seagal is the third of three actors credited before the title but leading lady, Jaime Pressly, was succinct about the reasons why she chose to do the film. "The fact that Tom Sizemore was in it. And Dennis Hopper. And the opportunity to work with both, I'd be a fool to pass." Ouch.

That's Tom Sizemore, whose 'Personal life' section on Wikipedia is now longer than the one on his 'Career', despite his having made well over 150 features. With supreme irony, given what's in that 'Personal life' section, he plays a narcotics cop here, Ray Nettles by name. At least he could bring some authenticity to the role; he's met enough narcotics cops.

And Dennis Hopper, who was only on set for one day. Sure, he's the overt villain of the piece as a Northern Irish bombmaker, Alex Swan, and he's everywhere in the film, but he shot all his scenes in a single day, which is seriously impressive. Seagal, whose Frank Glass is such a Zenlike bomb disposal expert that he may not actually breathe on screen, took six.

We meet Glass before the other core characters, because he's part of the opening action extravaganza. Terrorists have taken over a senator's mansion, which we only know is in upstate New York because that's what it says on screen in *Sweepers*, the 1998 Dolph Lundgren picture from which all this was lifted. The only new footage is someone telling Glass that it's all up to him but calling for more sharpshooters anyway and Seagal strutting slowly into the industrial complex that's supposed to be the senator's basement to disarm a bomb.

By the way, this is the context needed to understand why director Albert Pyun hates his own movie and has even apologised for it publicly more than once. The most explosive parts of his movie about explosives are literally not from his movie.

While Glass does disable that New York bomb, Swan blows the place up anyway with a different one, so we leap forward a year to San Francisco where Glass chills in a basement with his new bomb unit. That's TJ and Pooch and a cool chick with coloured hair, who collectively enjoy their bomb disposal robot and get upset when people mention the B word. Glass, of course, is waiting on the call that tells him that Swan is in town to blow shit up and Nettles, of course, makes that call because Swan's girl that he arrests at Fisherman's Wharf is wearing a bracelet made of semtex. Now we're moving.

Nettles is the cop here, doing all the legwork, and Seagal his mentor, somehow teaching him through osmosis the intuition needed to guess which wire to cut. This is odd because it means that Seagal provides the expertise in a picture that doesn't much value expertise because it never really solves anything. Both Sizemore and Seagal save respective days by guessing well. That's more important, especially when the bomb is a desktop computer and the wires go to the LEDs on the front.

It's also odd because it means that the action star in this action movie doesn't actually see much action until late in the movie. At least Ice T was happy about that. He shows up on a roof late in the picture for a couple of blink and you'll miss 'em moments, but long enough to have his arm snapped by Seagal. "That's what Steven Seagal does," he said. "He breaks limbs." To Ice T, that was a privilege and, in the context of the film, I can see that. Mostly Seagal is quiet. And sanctimonious.

By the way, Ice T isn't here much because his scenes are mostly not from this movie either. They're from another Dolph Lundgren movie, *The Peacekeeper*, which means that the helicopter shooting at a San Francisco roof was really shooting at a Chicago roof, but the roof in question was actually in Montreal anyway. This is why Pyun, post-*Ticker*, required in future contracts that he be given final cut on his movies. He's much happier nowadays.

Knowing how much of an action movie you're about to rent is actually spliced in from elsewhere would be useful knowledge to have, but it's rarely available beforehand. I tend to prejudge how bad an action movie is going to be by how many rappers feature in the cast. *Ticker* is a three rapper movie, but even that's misleading because none of them hang around for long. Nas is given more screen time than Ice T, as Art "Fuzzy" Rice, Detective Nettles's partner, but he's killed during their first interaction with Swan, so it isn't much more. Chilli doesn't get that much because she's only here to dance skankily in one scene. Well, she does play a drug-addicted prostitute.

There is an actual story here, but it's not particularly coherent. Swan is pissed at San Francisco's finest for arresting Claire, Pressly's character, so he wanders around the city blowing up pizza joints and bars until they give her back. Maybe he thinks they're judging his Irish accent. I certainly was. Nettles chases around like a madman to stop him while Glass chills and offers advice. Frankly, Seagal could have been replaced by a fortune cookie, as long as that fortune cookie could break Ice T's arm.

There is a decent twist, which would have generated some praise for the film had it not sucked so painfully otherwise. As it is, I'll remember this one for being an action movie that borrowed its action; a Dennis Hopper movie in which he mostly interacts with actors who weren't actually there at the time; and a Steven Seagal movie in which he doesn't swear much and tries not to move.

–Hal CF Astell

Half Past Dead (2002)

Half Past Dead has a plot that is almost too good for Seagal. Seagal plays Sasha Petrosevitch, an undercover cop in a prison trying to get information on who killed his wife. He just so happens to stumble across a plot where a death-row inmate, Lester, is wanted by a group called the 49ner's. Lester has information about the location of a lot of gold. Lester is executed that night, which brings me to a side point: this prison is tricked out, the writer, Don Michael Paul, created a prison where the guards treat the inmates more humanely. Also, and I don't know why this is a nice touch, the inmate gets to decide how he dies. I thought that was a nice touch. It also uses the plot element of a re-opened Alcatraz. I almost wanted to say that they stole this concept from *The Rock*, which was made six years earlier, however in this film, Alcatraz is re-opened and has prisoners. Also, *The Rock* deals with people who are inexperienced. In this one, everyone is trained. By the end of the movie, it felt like the only true comparison was that it was set on Alcatraz.

Anywho, this is a PG-13 rated Steven Seagal movie. The action is toned down, but somehow still better choreographed than most of his R-rated fare. The story is basic, run of the mill, but performance quality from some of the supporting roles is amazing. Bruce Weitz, who plays the inmate Lester and thus the target of the group, has a simple role, be the human version of capture the flag, however he is so calm, perhaps it's him accepting his fate. What a lot of people both in the world of the film and in the audience didn't think about is this, what would you do, if you knew you were dead either way, that's an idea he has, when he does his final act in the film, which by the time it comes, I had more sympathy for, than I had planned on. The writing on this film was good, Seagal would later go on to do films with much worse writing and between this movie, which was released in 2002, and *Machete* which was released in 2010, all his films would be direct-to-video. My only real complaint with this movie, is how gold is represented. Gold is a heavy metal, if you want hundreds of millions of dollars in gold, that will weigh thousands of pounds and not easily transported, DUH!

Seagal got himself a good cast. Some of the other casting in this film is Morris Chestnut, who plays the leader of the 49ners and thus goes by the name 49NER-1. I will simply address him as Chestnut since his characters real name is Donny Johnson. It's funny to see Chestnut on this side of Seagal since the last time they teamed up was *Under Siege 2: Dark Territory*, where they were on the same side and Chestnut was just an employee on a train.

Tony Plana plays the prison warden in effective scenes as well. Stephen J. Canell plays the head of the Federal Bureau of Prisons in a nice longer cameo. In an attempt at racial equality, a lot of the prisoners are Black and played by Ja Rule and Kurupt. There is an awesome scene where an inmate has a rocket launcher of some kind and he points it at Ja Rule, who quickly smacks it away, and this happens a couple of times, its a gag seen several times in movies before, but with prisoners, the gag feels a little fresher. Seagal then teaches the prisoner how to use the rocket launcher, now for visual reference, the one holding the rocket is launcher is a tiny man in terms of build, so he goes flying through a window when the rocket it launched, when the prisoners pick him back up, he simply says "what a rush." The prisoners are played with dignity and humor, and it shows.

Seagal's role doesn't require much acting. He just has to accept that he is in prison and try to get the information about his wife's murder. He then has to pick up guns or whatever he has to use and fend off terrorists on the island. He does have a funny exchange with Lester when he meets him and they have a quick discussion and then Lester flat out asks if Sasha wants to know why Lester is there, Sasha gives the quickest "no" ever put on film, Lester ignores it and tells him anyway, which is good for the audience's sake because it's where we get our needed exposition. It was a funny interaction that really sets the characters. This element would mostly go bye-bye in later Seagal films. You can tell Seagal had some fun playing this part, it's nice to have him do even a scene with some comedy, where there is no body count. He doesn't joke about killing people who deep philosophy of preservation of life, he will just teach someone how to use a rocket launcher. I liked the roles with a calmer Seagal, or as calm as he could be. Chestnut did what he could with his run-of-the-mill villain role. I wish his motive was deeper than money.

The fight scenes are what you expect, they would lose a significant amount of quality in later films, where Seagal just lost interest in what he was doing to the point that he would take supporting roles where he just simply shoots people instead of his martial arts. *Half Past Dead* is actually one of the more enjoyable early 2000s forays. I would chalk this up to a guilty pleasure for his films. It wasn't new in terms of motive, but new takes on an old concept are always welcomed in my book.

–Stephen Kessen

Out for a Kill (2003)

Out for Justice and *Hard to Kill* are two of the more successful flicks in Steven Seagal's filmography. Therefore, titling a lesser effort *Out for a Kill* was a smart move from a commercial perspective. If you had to stumble upon this movie randomly, you'd be forgiven for mistaking it for a sequel to either of these masterpieces. The producers were probably relying on these lapses in judgment from action aficionados to make any money off the film as well. The questionable quality of *Out for a Kill* was never going to propel the actor back to genre superstardom, after all.

Directed by *The Mercenary*'s Michael Oblowitz, from a script by Dennis Dimster and Danny Lerner, *Out for a Kill* sees Seagal play Professor Robert Burns. He's an archaeologist whose contributions to the field have earned him Yale University's prestigious Winthrop Award for Excellence. All is going well for the professor until he's sent on an expedition to China. There, he uncovers a mysterious artifact and finds himself framed for drug smuggling.

The situation intensifies when Burns gets released from prison. The authorities want to use him as bait to lure the bigger fish out of the shadows. The Triads obviously want the professor dead for exposing their operation. So, they send hitmen after him and his family. Unfortunately, his wife gets caught in the crossfire (or an explosion, to be more specific). With nothing left to lose and vengeance on his agenda, Burns sets out for a kill.

While no one goes into a direct-to-video Seagal movie expecting quality, this one is a reminder of how far the once-mighty action star had fallen by 2003. *Out for a Kill* embellishes some of the worst qualities of the actor's B-grade fare, but that doesn't mean the film is a worthless way to kill 80 minutes either. It certainly isn't boring.

Let's get the negative aspects out of the way first. The special effects are abysmal. *Out for a Kill* supposedly takes place in the human realm, but this a world where people seem trapped in a virtual hellscape. Given that virtual reality and similar concepts don't inform the plot in any way, there's no telling why the filmmakers chose to make everything appear so simulated.

Of course, this element of the film probably wouldn't be as bad if the effects weren't so amateurish. The reported budget for *Out for a Kill* was $14 million, but most of that money was probably spent on Seagal's buffet bill. The production values are nothing to write home about even by Seagal's usual DTV standards. If the Sci-Fi channel made action movies in the early 2000s, they'd look like this.

One standout scene features computer-generated bullets piercing a vehicle in slow-motion. It wouldn't seem out of place in a bad Playstation 2 shooter game. Instead of trying to disguise the poor effects work, though, *Out for a Kill* embraces these shortcomings with a sense of show-off pride. Perhaps the filmmakers were just excited by the tools they had at their disposal and decided to experiment a bit too much. Some viewers will feel dizzy watching the craziness unfold.

The CGI overload is at its funniest during the emotional moments. Burns' wife's death is particularly noteworthy. Prior to the explosion, which boasts some very non-convincing flames, there is a gloomy lightning storm that tries to evoke a sense of impending despair. As Burns watches the explosion, memories of his now-dead spouse come flooding back to him in the form of cartoonish family heirlooms. Watching Seagal trying to showcase emotion amid the fake fire and roaring sky is an experience, though.

One can only assume that Seagal's contract only required the actor to show up for a certain amount of days and be done with the picture afterward. He clearly didn't lend his talents to the post-production process. The film features some inner monologues from Burns that sound nothing like the actor playing him. The voice actor doesn't even try to impersonate Seagal.

These technical malfunctions are also supplemented with a story that's unnecessarily stuffed and incoherent. *Out for a Kill* keeps introducing ideas to the mix in the hope that some of them might land, but few actually do. Burns is a professor who suddenly becomes a one-man killing machine. To explain this, he's given a mysterious backstory halfway through the movie, but it's never fully developed.

The movie also takes a brief excursion into the fantastical territory for a fight sequence involving a wolf-like Chinese butcher who can crawl up walls. It's far from the most impressive physical altercation in Seagal's oeuvre, but there's enough nonsensical goofiness on display to make for some entertaining viewing. No one enters a movie like this expecting logic, but Out for a Kill offers no context as to why moments like this exist.

Seagal's stunt double is tasked with carrying out the bulk of the action, and he's barely disguised in several scenes. But there are some moments of carnage that are adequately choreographed. The highlight is a sword fight that sees the central professor-cum-vigilante throw down with some monks at a funeral. The rogue's gallery of assassins is actually quite varied too, even though some are nothing more than Asian stereotypes.

The script, meanwhile, is loaded with great lines. These incorporate everything fortune cookie philosophizing to tough-guy action movie bravado. "If he's innocent, the Pope wears panties," states a detective who wants to lock the professor behind bars and throw away the key. If you think that's a good line, you'll have fun with *Out for a Kill.*

Most Seagal connoisseurs have learned to find nuggets of gold in movies that most film fans regard as sewage. *Out for a Kill* won't offend the sensibilities of those who have stuck with the actor following his commercial decline. This is a terrible movie and a career-low point for

Vladimir Putin's favorite American action star. But those who search for beauty in trainwrecks might fall for its low-rent charms. Enter at your own risk.

–Kieran Fisher

Belly of the Beast (2003)

Siu-Ting Ching is arguably the most accomplished filmmaker Steven Seagal has ever worked with. Andew Davis, who directed Seagal in *Above the Law* and *Under Siege*, may have gone to receive an Oscar nomination for his work on *The Fugitive*, but Ching has two Golden Horse Awards—often called "China's Oscars"—and three Hong Kong Film Awards.

It's no surprise, then, that Ching gives us a masterful mix of grand storytelling, Eastern mysticism, tragic romance, and brilliantly choreographed martial arts.

Unfortunately, he gives us all this in his 1987 film *A Chinese Ghost Story*. His 2003 Seagal picture *Belly of the Beast* attempts a similar combination with far less success.

Here, Seagal practically yawns every line as a former CIA agent, now retired following an undercover clusterfuck that saw his partner accidentally kill an innocent civilian. Said partner, played by Byron Mann (Ryu in the enjoyably cheesy 1994 *Street Fighter* movie) also retired, swearing off violence in order to seek atonement at a Buddhist monastery.

Everything changes, though, when Seagal's daughter—who just happens to be best friends with the daughter of a prominent U.S. Senator—is kidnapped by Thai terrorists. *Or is she?* There are a lot of muddled attempts at political intrigue and "shocking" plot twists that never make much sense, but the important thing is that Seagal has to pull a Liam Neeson and travel to Thailand on a roaring rampage of revenge to rescue his doting daughter.

So far, so mundane. The first hint we get that this isn't a typical Seagal actioner is when, during a fight with a group of thugs at a fish market, a mysterious man with what a suspiciously wizard-esque beard and a faintly glowing forehead tattoo is shown watching from the shadows.

His gaze is enough to send the same thug Seagal is interrogating into hysterics, leading to a decidedly *Final Destination*-y death wherein said thug slips on a tomato, causing him to go careering across a countertop face-first into a meat cleaver.

Later, a seemingly entranced woman wanders out in front of Seagal's car, narrowly avoiding becoming roadkill. Of course, without a moment's hesitation Seagal understands that he's supposed to get out of the car and follow her into the backroom of a tavern, where she can take off her top so that a hidden message can magically appear on her tits. What?!?

Finally, in the film's third act, all these brief moments of WTF-ness explode into the foreground, as the forehead-tattooed beardo from earlier is revealed to be a practitioner of *barang*—AKA "Thai voodoo." While our hero engages another character in a shockingly good sword vs. spear smackdown—shades of the Jet Li/Donnie Yen battle from 2004's wuxia epic *Hero*, which Ching choreographed—said sorcerer drives pins into a doll made out of clothing stolen from Seagal's hotel room.

Luckily, Seagal receives mystical assistance of his own courtesy of Mann's Buddhist monk brethren, who repel the black magic baddie in what can only be described as a "prayer fight."

As a blatant bid by a veteran Chinese director to break into the U.S. market with a convoluted low-budget direct-to-video potboiler starring a visibly disinterested and past-his-prime Seagal, *Belly of the Beast* has plenty of issues. Mann's performance is a highlight, but his character seems a little too willing to renounce his pacifist vows the moment Seagal comes calling. Most of the other cast members, meanwhile, appear to have been hired for their interesting faces rather than their acting abilities.

Worst of all, one of the script's only female characters exists almost solely to have a deeply uncomfortable sex scene with Seagal, which takes place shortly after she find the bloody corpse of her murdered roommate. Ick.

Nevertheless, thanks to a few different factors, *Belly of the Beast* is a minor gem in Seagal's latter-day filmography. The decision to shoot on-location in Thailand gives the production a sense of scope and authenticity, and Ching's direction is very polished and stylish. Additionally, his background as a fight choreographer produces some genuinely great action scenes—most notably the aforementioned sword/spear duel, a John Woo-esque trainyard shootout, a kinetic faceoff with a razor-clawed *kathoey* (!), and a short but satisfying sequence where Seagal beats the shit out of almost an entire police station *while handcuffed.*

What really makes *Belly of the Beast* stand out, though, is its weirdness.

Unlike many of his peers, during the '80s/'90s golden age of action movies, Seagal never really branched out from his comfort zone of street-level crime stories and anti-terrorist thrillers. Alternatively, Schwarzenegger mastered everything from sci-fi to sword-and-sorcery to comedy, while Stallone always had the integrity of the *Rocky* series to fall back on. Even fellow B-listers Jean-Claude Van Damme, Dolph Lundgren, and Chuck Norris broke up their action-heavy filmographies with genre-bending hybrids like *The Minion, Timecop,* and *Hellbound.*

Being the first Seagal picture with overt, undeniable supernatural themes—yes, the villains in *Marked for Death* used Haitian voodoo imagery but only as a scare tactic, and the Native American vision quest in *On Deadly Ground* was ambiguously framed as a hallucination—gives *Belly of the Beast* a campy batshit charm that recalls Ching's roots with Shaw Brothers Studio.

Although there is a clear attempt to reign in the film's more eccentric impulses, either by the director himself or—more likely—someone on the *gwai lo* side of this Hong Kong/UK/Canada co-production, *Belly of the Beast*'s greatest weakness isn't that it's too weird. It's that it's not weird enough. In other words, it would have benefited greatly from more prayer fights and magic tits, and fewer conspiratorial double-crosses.

As it is, *Belly of the Beast* exists as a fitfully entertaining schlockbuster that represents "what could have been." While Seagal would occasionally delve into quirkier fare as his career spiraled deeper into DTV obscurity (see *Today You Die*, *Against the Dark*, *The Perfect Weapon*, etc.), most of his movies have remained interchangeable.

It begs the question: what if he experimented more? Challenged himself more? Tried to broaden his audience more? Instead of simply remaking the same handful of movies over and over again, could there someday be a Steven Seagal version of *JCVD*?

At this point, is it too late?

−William Tea

Clementine (2004)

We should preface this with a simple disclaimer that the great Sensei Steven Seagal is barely in this film clocking in at roughly ten minutes of total screen time, but somehow as a secondary antagonist he finds a way to leave his mark on the film and score what was inevitably a very easy payday for himself. I would love to tell you that this was a quality piece of film, but it very assuredly is not. This started as a glowing review for this awful film because that is the specialty of this lowly writer; terrible D-list movies that are terrible in the best kind of way, but this is different. This film is not on the level of a Tommy Wiseau masterpiece but rather finds itself lost in an identity crisis of deciding what it should be.

Clementine is a Korean film that released in 2004 but based on how the characterization is done, the story is presented, and film is paced you would be remiss to believe that this came out in the 2000's rather than in the late 80's as a direct competition to films like *Best of the Best* or *The Kickboxer*, albeit still inferior to all of those. The film follows the main character Kim (played by Dong-Jun Lee) who is a former taekwondo champion fighter until he loses a rigged fight. This is a rather common trope with stories like this but to add to the drama, not only does he lose this fight that is taking place in Las Vegas but conveniently his wife dies during childbirth and his brand-new daughter is then put into an orphanage. Being that I am American, this seems ridiculous even by our standards, but that is neither here nor there. The plus side is that he gets his daughter back and decides to walk away from his violent life of fighting and becomes a police officer. And they lived happily ever after. Except that would be too easy.

Kim has all the skills that he would need to be a successful police officer so the change in career really seems like a natural fit and a good way to get away from the shady fighting life he had been so accustomed to. The main problem is that as the old adage goes "it's tough to teach an old dog new tricks." Kim is certainly skilled at taking down bad guys, but perhaps a little too good as he quickly finds himself getting in trouble for being too violent. He beats up a group of gangsters and when he is told to apologize for the use of excessive force he goes and beats them up again. As i'm sure you can imagine this leads to his removal from the police force. But once again by sheer happenstance and coincidence the gangs boss happened to be around when his thugs got beat up and he saw nothing but dollar signs. Boss man offers Kim big bucks to return to fighting and now that Kim has found himself jobless with a daughter to take care of he has no choice but to accept the offer and enter in to a plethora of underground fights that are one hundred percent not legal, but also one hundred percent more acceptable use his certain set of skills. I would be remiss to not mention though that he wasn't given much of a choice in the matter. This wasn't just about providing for his daughter, but also making sure that she was safe and alive because bossman decides that kidnapping the daughter is the only way to make sure that Kim complies. All in all, standard business practice.

We are quickly reminded of how good of a fighter Kim is as he plows his way through the competitors that are thrown in front of him, but much like the beginning of the film we are again presented with a fixed fight; one that Kim is expected to lose in order to ensure his daughters safety. This is when our hero (note: definitely not the hero in this film) Jack Miller, played by the great sensei himself Steven Seagal comes into the picture. He is an undefeated fighter and Kim's boss stands to make a lot of money with Kim losing to Jack. As they have what can only be described as a lackluster-ly epic fight, we see that Kim's daughter has been saved and once noticing this Kim is free to go all out and win the fight. This "win" is no doubt debatable since he is a bloody mess and ends up stretchered to the hospital, but the movie ends on a happy note as The Great One comes to visit Kim in the hospital and we are left with a happy bro moment between two fighters as well as a very wholesome smiling moment featuring Kim and his daughter.

Clementine is by no stretch of the imagination a fantastic movie. As I started at the beginning of this, it would have done much better if it was released at a time that it would have been relevant, but even that could be debated. The cast would have been much different, choice pieces of film would have been much more competitive, but ultimately, Seagal would have been much younger, leading to better fights and likely more screen time. It's a give and take that will be debated by the film community for years to come. Or at the very least, will be debated by those that have chosen to get this book and learn all about one of the best film libraries of our time.

–Corey Maslowski

Out of Reach (2004)

Out of Reach stars Steven Seagal as a nature survivalist, who was once the ultimate badass. He has a teenage pen pal that he financially supports through the orphanage. This movie did not age well; however, it was probably done in an effort to make the movie more interesting, it fails in such spectacularly bad fashion. There is early talk in the movie about a cypher, so you know that will come back later. The foster home that his pen pal is in, is actually used for human trafficking. So Seagal sits back and lets the feds take care to it, I am totally messing with you, he goes on a one-man band to kill every last person who had anything to do with it.

The first thing I noticed about this movie is how terrible his voice is dubbed. Many claim that changes were made to the plot after the movie was filmed, that's right, they fucked it up in post. The dubber doesn't even try to mimic his voice or his mumble. It sounds clear as day and about 15 years younger. It also reverts back to Steven's normal voice in some scenes, creating a distraction in this movie. I would do this entire essay on the poor duding choice. Most of this film contains voiceover it can. The only thing that is worth a damn is the cinematography. It does a good job of using master shots and sequencing overhead shots. I feel bad that the cinematographer who would be shooting more tv drama is working on his film. The writing doesn't even try to be original. Yes, the main villain actually has to answer to someone about his operation. Most action films contain villains who like to fence or who like to play chess in an effort to show their intellectual advantage, this movie does both. The dialogue in this film is on the nose. It also contains the great line "with these guns, I can't kill you slowly, and I'd like to." Yes, you can in fact kill people slowly with guns, you just have to miss all vital organs. There were sometimes I could mouth the characters next lines. The direction is nothing but shit.

Characters who have complete vantage points of a room don't notice a character next to a wall, and act surprised when Seagal grabs him. Why does a henchmen have time to shoot the woman next to Seagal, and yet not enough time to fire at him, while he flips a desk over, the light will break, giving the gunman total darkness to deal with, the lighting is also pointless, since the lights are on in other places. This is my first time ever bitching about set design.

The first 20 minutes contain no excitement whatsoever. Even the kidnapping scene, which are almost impossible to screw up, lack enthusiasm. The editing is ridiculous. Seagal sees two men who are sent to kill him, he closes the door, and walks in the opposite direction from the bathroom. The bad guys bust in and see a bathroom shower with steam and a suit in there. I know literally nothing about science, but there is no way that shower will get that hot, that quickly. the same scene later features a death sequence of a man falling out of a window, that is so poorly edited, it looks like he magically switches front to back before falling onto the top of a car. It picks up but is much quieter than Seagal's normal fare. I also reviewed *Gutshot Straight*, which also uses less violence and has more of a criminal element. The filmmakers should have hopped in a time machine, went to the future, took notes, and re-wrote most of the screenplay. I know I am asking for a lot that's not possible. Seagal tries to make action movies about issues going on, like the environment or in this case, human trafficking, but when the script is this bland, it's almost a disservice to the cause. I wonder what issue he will take on with his next film. I know he was beaten to the punch when it comes to police brutality, but maybe he can take on Russian meddling in the elections set in 2024. As I typed that sentence, while venting my rage on this keyboard, I realized, I would actually love to see it. You could have lame ass jokes about Rocky or something. Maybe he could tackle mail-in voting and beat the guy's head in with a mailbox. He can also grab an envelope and paper cut someone a thousand times.

I want to say good things about this movie, but I also don't want to lie. The cinematography is above average, as I stated before. Also, this movie's run time is 80 minutes before the credits roll.

Let's bitch about Seagal shall we? I don't think it's fair that his voice is dubbed. I can't make fun of his cadence, if I instantly know that it's someone else, and boy will you. Seagal has to "act" more than most of his films here because the plot doesn't allow him to fight or kill everything he can see. He tries to show emotion, but it comes out as blank. He has an impossible task to make his lines interesting, his fighting moves tack a backseat next to getting face to face with people and having a conversation. The only person who gives a weaker performance is Ida Nowakowska, who plays his pen pal. She isn't given much to do in the film and when she is ultimately rescued, she seems as about as frustrated with what took him so long as opposed to actually being rescued. Now Ida Nowakowska is a dancer and not much of an actress, as she would go on to do more short films and dance videos. Seagal and her don't have much chemistry. I spent so much time going… WHY?

–Stephen Kessen

Into the Sun (2005)

You may say, "well this wasn't Segal's greatest performance and you can't judge him solely on one movie alone."

As it's the only movie I ever plan on watching with Segal in it, I say, "watch me."

"What the fuck is an American doing swinging around a sword"

Well, my doomed friend, I asked myself that same question from the opening scene where Travis Hunter (played by the personality-challenged, Steven Seagal) interacts with a samurai sword fanboy. I've never seen a Steven Segal movie in my life, likely by deliberate design. I do however like to live deliciously. Full disclosure, I thought this movie was set in an American city until about half-way through this film because why would it be set anywhere else? Nothing about this move screams Japanese culture or strict practices, so it could have been set anywhere with where Japanese gangs might have influence.

What could have been a fish out of water film for any other Japanese/ Japanese-American actor saddled with a stan like Steven Seagal who thinks he's a ninja, we're instead left with actual Steven Segal believing he can co-opt another culture in full black trench coat and sword. He thinks affectations help him blend, as only an oblivious White, cis-het man will do, but in a culture as traditionally xenophobic as Japan, it only serves to hammer home Segal's appropriation. He's not cooler for learning Japanese. He's not cooler for pretending to be a native and speaking the language. He's everything wrong with a certain subset of White men trying to colonize their fetish.

Okay, so let's get this shitshow started.

"This kills very well"

In *Into the Sun* (2005) the FBI (American) calls the CIA (also American) to interfere in a murder mystery on Japanese soil. That's it. That's the movie. This is where any rational individual turns off the movie and scrolls aimlessly through their Netflix queue for an hour.

Anyway, enter CIA operative Travis Hunter (Steven Seagal), who's deep cover identity is apparently a dealer of Japanese stuff he finds and then sells back to actual Japanese people. Some Seagal ego-stroking later, you know because he sooooooooooo good at Japanese stuff (because he's so immersed in the culture, he's practically invisible) he walks into an CIA building completely unchallenged, proving he's also an American and no one tells him no. All to this is establish that Travis Hunter is swinging the biggest of American dicks (in Japan) and isn't just cool, but always well-lit and a "Badass".

For someone undercover, Travis generally makes his presence known by simply existing as a 6'4" White American. He's an operative everyone knows and anyone can find. He's been tapped to look into the assassination of a Tokyo's Governor in the most ham-handed investigation the outside of the *Bad Boys* franchise. People are murdered left and right as a wildly erratic young Yakuza guns start eliminating the old Yakuza guard and other competition for the coveted smuggling heroin-in-fish export trade lanes. Travis is given an FBI liaison, Special Agent Sean Mac (Matthew Davis) who knows nothing about the FBI or CIA or being an agent. He's a moron, who like Hunter, believes that being mediocre and American allows him access everywhere he's not wanted. It gets him killed and hat's not a spoiler, it's the natural order of things. Travis doesn't find the Yakuza, they find him, everywhere, and the story progresses solely without him and essentially is resolved with a minimal amount of his meddling.

"Eat your chopsticks"

It's not uncommon for an American Action Hero to try to emulate the strict Asian disciplines that keep them in shape and focused. I'm thinking specifically the of Marvel comic character Blade. We see those influences in his fighting style and how he conducts himself. It's not only his aesthetic, it makes up Blade's whole being.

We don't have that with Travis Hunter.

For a film he's supposedly rewritten and starred in, Seagal shoehorned a character in a movie that doesn't need him. His actions are incidental because the heavy lifting is done by everyone else. Travis Hunter mostly lumbers through scenes, speaking Japanese (sure) and fighting (sort of). His entire character is "knows the culture and prefers a sword", but it makes him neither an action hero nor a protagonist we feel like rooting for. It makes him a poser.

Seagal created a Gary Stu, someone whose seen his favorite action heroes fight, fall in love, lose his love and go on a revenge-filled rampage to avenge the woman he's lost. None of that is in this movie. The plot is convoluted and over complicated, and the editing is so poor with tiny clips of two-sentence dialogue they advance nothing and only highlight Seagal's fetish for Japan and the Japanese culture.

"both uttering karate cries"

Travis Hunter is given with a super creepy relationship with Nayako (Kanako Yamaguchi), a woman literally half his age. They have sex on bamboo mats, by which I mean she gets naked, so for the good of humanity, she has to die. It's as ham-handed as the rest of the movie and Seagal's so emotionless, both during his courtship, the "sex", and after his fiancé gets fridged, it's not even laughable.

I mean, it's actually kinda gross.

"To My American Bitch"

The Japanese criminals get all of the cheesy one-liners. They have to, because criminal psychopaths can only be crazy yet darkly humored. They survive by being wild, so the young Yakuza and their temporary cohorts, the Chinese Tonks join forces to become immeasurably and

Hollywood wealthy. Crazy, erratic and borderline psychotic can only end in stable wealth and longevity.

There is no rhyme or reason to what some lines are in English and some are in Japanese. I know a lot of American romanization has crept into Japanese, but the script is just baffling.

"See You in Hell."

If *Into the Sun* teaches us anything, and we have to believe we're being punished to learn a specific lesson, it's that being a White guy in a foreign country guarantees you freedom from consequences. It makes you invisible, though you stick out like an abandoned truck on blocks in someone's front yard. Colonialism is acceptable and necessary because you're American and nothing can stop you. You're worthy because you exist, not because you've earned anything.

I guess it explains why there are over 60 Steven Seagal movies.

Can I go now?

–Montilee Stormer

Submerged (2005)

When Patton Oswalt was a guest on *The Pete Holmes Show*, he was asked about his role in *Blade: Trinity* (2004). Oswalt stated, "If you just sit and watch *Blade: Trinity*, it's a D-minus. It just doesn't work. But if you know what they went through to get that movie made, it is an A-plus. The fact that movie exists puts it above *Citizen Kane*." He would explain that David S Goyer, the writer/director, had his hands full with Wesley Snipes, the star of the movie, who was reportedly beyond difficult to work with during filming. The relationship between writer/director Anthony 'Tony' Hickox and Steven Seagal during the filming of *Submerged* (2005) was a very similar experience. However, to consider *Submerged* a D-minus effort is beyond generous. It teases the viewer with hopes of a submarine film, but pulls the rug out quickly, and feeds the viewer Hickox's utterly ridiculous half-baked Tom Clancy plot covered with a thick gravy of Seagal's egotistical nonsense.

Submarine films should be exciting because they are set on these amazing weapons of utter destruction and terror lurking deep in the ocean, but they are also set on these incredibly vulnerable vessels deep in the ocean. Two fine examples are *Das Boot* and *The Hunt for Red October*. *Das Boot* is Wolfgang Peterson's 1981 World War II epic adventure while *The Hunt for Red October* is John McTiernan's 1990 Cold War thriller featuring Sean Connery and his missing-in-action Russian accent.

Submerged started off as an interesting concept where a submarine crew, led by a grizzled old captain, would experience an alien-like presence on their vessel. Hickox's vision according to the Unofficial Steven Seagal Page was "*The Thing* meets *Das Boot*". Once the script was completed, the movie moved forward with Seagal starring in the role of the captain. Hickox claimed that Seagal was very receptive to his idea when they met, but Seagal went over Hickox's head and demanded the script be changed because he wasn't interested in starring in a monster movie. *Submerged* became a direct-to-video feature that is a submarine movie in name only. It follows Chris Kody (Seagal) and his wrongly accused band of mercenaries as they attempt to stop a mad scientist and his sinister mind control project.

Hickox was no rookie in the industry. He was the writer/director for *Waxwork* (1988) and *Waxwork II* (1992), plus he directed other films such as *Hellraiser III* (1992) and *The Contaminated Man* (2000). His father was Douglas Hickox, a career assistant director and director. His mother was Anne V. Coates, editor numerous films such as *Lawrence of Arabia* (1962) and *The Elephant Man* (1980). She won the Academy Award in 1963 for her work on *Lawrence of Arabia* and was awarded a BAFTA fellowship along with a Lifetime Achievement Academy Award. The ball was in Hickox's court to appease Seagal and he did that by re-writing the script for *Submerged*.

The story turned into an action thriller where United States Government discovers a rogue scientist named Lehder (Nick Brimble) is in Uruguay working with corrupt members of the military to oust the president. Lehder can brainwash people using a special device and he can mobilize them remotely via cell phone to carry out his evil deeds. A US Special Forces unit tries to stop Lehder, but they are captured, and brainwashed.

In a last minute 'Hail Mary' attempt at saving the day, the US Government authorizes a group of incarcerated mercenaries led by Kody to go in and defeat Lehder with a promise of money and a full pardon if successful. Years ago, Kody and his crew protected Maui from terrorists that had commandeered a tanker full of explosives. Sadly, the overly powerful and soulless United Nations decided to throw Kody and his buddies in jail on some trumped up charges, which is absolute John Birch Society rubbish.

Kody fails to capture Lehder but rescues the US Special Forces unit. A submarine is hijacked by Kody and his crew to transport themselves and the US Special Forces unit to a Navy ship in international waters. While on the submarine, the US Special Forces unit tries to kill Kody and his crew but are eliminated. The Navy fears Kody's submarine has been taken over by the brainwashed soldiers, so for some odd reason, they launch a missile to take out the submarine. Kody and his crew abandon ship and return to Uruguay to finish the job against Lehder.

Lehder shows up negotiating with an international tech company in Uruguay to continue his work in ousting the president. Apparently, the president hates the tech company, which is grounds for a *coup d'état*. Lehder discovers he can access the tech company's bank account and decides to steal hundreds of millions from them, leave the country, and retire to an island. Everything culminates during an opera attended by the president. Allegedly, the opera scene was one of Seagal's demands when the script was rewritten. Interestingly enough, it is perhaps the best sequence in the movie. Lehder is killed and the movie ends.

Submerged went from an interesting horror movie to an almost unwatchable action film. Bad writing and Seagal's antics sunk this effort. Twenty minutes are spent on a submarine and the whole sequence comes off as a compromise. Seagal stays seated most of the time he's on the sub, and he's seated for a fight scene. Not long after Kody is introduced, the overdubbing work from another actor begins. Allegedly, Seagal refused to do post-production work, so the end result is two different voices for Kody. We're not talking a few lines, but a majority of Seagal's lines. There appears to be no research conducted for this film. Kody's crew is told to meet at the ancient Mayan ruins in Uruguay, but that civilization was never in South America. Also, Uruguay is confused with Argentina during the dictatorship of Juan Peron. This was definitely hard to watch.

–Tony Doug Wright

Today You Die (2005)

My new stepson, who is now 10, often reminisces about an action movie he made on his mom's phone when he was eight that he wrote, directed, and starred in. I have often wondered what exactly that might look like. After having watched *Today You Die*, I'm fairly sure it looks a lot like that (only probably a little bit better). All film people know that Steven Seagal movies are not a place one goes to find quality, but even with that in mind, *Today You Die* is an impressively (and aggressively) bad movie. Where most bad films are really only truly bad in regards to one or two aspects, *Today You Die* has the distinction of being bad in pretty much every way possible. It's telling when Steven Seagal is one of the best things about a movie.

By this point in his career, Seagal was already starting to decline physically. His face looks leathery and bloated, he has a widow's peak that would make Eddie Munster jealous, and his hair looks like straw jutting out from the back of his head. He is, of course, emotionless throughout the proceedings and it's immediately clear that he's just phoning in his performance here, which is terrible even by Steven Seagal standards. He also wears a jacket through most of the film, obviously trying to conceal how plump he'd become. (This is hilariously apparent in prison scenes, where Seagal is the only prisoner wearing a jacket. The prison must have known how special this prisoner was, because even his undershirt is different from every other prisoner's standard-issue garb.)

With *Today You Die*, director Don E. Fontleroy and crew did something interesting; they almost managed to make Seagal look like a halfway decent actor (even with him sleepwalking through the film) by surrounding him with actors who are even worse performers than he is. Sarah Buxton is easily the worst performer in this film. When Seagal acts in scenes alongside Buxton, she makes him look like Laurence Olivier by comparison. The producers were clearly hoping to duplicate the minimal success of the 2002 film *Half Past Dead*, which teamed Seagal up with rapper Ja Rule. This time out, Seagal hams it up alongside Naughty By Nature's Treach. It turns out that, while Treach is a highly skilled rapper, he is a terrible actor. So, while Seagal is a pretty horrendous actor, he is somehow a better actor than Treach. Although, to be fair, I'd bet dollars to doughnuts that Treach is a better rapper than Seagal.

It's probably not fair to say everyone in the film is bad. There are some solid veteran actors in the mix with Nick Mancuso, Robert Miano, and Kevin Tighe, but none of them appear on screen long enough to do much. It's likely that they were each hired for a mere day or two of filming. There are some interesting cameos to note here. Chloe Grace Moretz pops up in an early appearance here but does little more than appear on screen. MMA fighter Randy Couture also shows up just long enough to get pummeled by Seagal.

The filmmaking and editing of this film are really, really poor. No doubt director Fauntleroy and editor Robert Ferretti were trying to make this look like a big-budget Tony Scott-type actioner, but they failed miserably. The overuse of slow-mo shots is side-splittingly funny, and the weird editing style is a wonder to behold; Ferretti constantly does this thing where he excises several seconds of footage, making the characters jump ahead a couple seconds. This technique has worked in other films with bigger budgets and better editors, but here it just looks silly and low rent. But it's hardly out of place; everything about *Today You Die* feels low-rent. It's weird because there are helicopters and explosions and a soundtrack featuring a Frank Sinatra tune (although some shots were edited in from other films), so there was obviously some sort of budget. But if this is the case, then why weren't better, more talented filmmakers brought in to make this film presentable?

All of the dialogue feels improvised, like the actors just winged it on set (although there are two screenwriters credited). And the plot is a terrible mishmash of mediocre ideas that worked better in other films. The plot is basically that Seagal is a robber who is set up with a supposedly straight job to drive an armored car containing $20 million. But Seagal is then set up and leads the cops on a high-speed armored car chase through Las Vegas, which sounds a hell of a lot more interesting than it really is. All of this leads to Seagal going to prison, where he meets Treach. He and Treach have no reason to be close friends, but they inexplicably become comrades almost immediately. They then escape from and Seagal sets out for vengeance, snapping arms and legs and whispering awful lines of dialogue right and left.

To give you an idea just how bad this movie is, I'm going to describe two scenes. In one, Seagal fights the man who tricked him into driving the armored car. During the fight, it appears that Seagal is throwing around a completely different guy who is wearing a wig. In another scene, Seagal and Treach are driving and having a conversation. For some reason, it looks suspiciously as though each side of the conversation was shot separately. I might be wrong about both of these scenes, but it's a testament to how crappy the film looks that a viewer would have reason to wonder.

–Andrew J. Rausch

Black Dawn (2005)

The best part about *Black Dawn*? It ended.

Hah! Okay, it's not that bad. Despite myself, I actually started off enjoying the movie. Right off the bat, we're told this is from Andrew Stevens Entertainment, which almost ensures it'll be terrible. It starts in a fast-paced manner, as an arms dealer played by John Pyper-Ferguson pays Seagal (as the improbably-named "Jonathan Cold") to break his also-an-arms-dealer brother out of prison. (I was embarrassed that Pyper-Ferguson was in this. Sort of ruined the memory of "Pete's piece" (from *The Adventures of Brisco County Jr.*) for me. So goddamn you – GODDAMN YOU ALL TO HELL! – for making me watch it.)

The movie starts with grainy footage – sometimes color, sometimes black-and-white. There's some bombing plot going on, as two terrorist ringleaders meet to discuss it. One of the men is assassinated by a sniper, after which the other man and his pals steal a mysterious briefcase from some uniformed guys. Then we jump into a fairly standard story of Cold – a disavowed former CIA operative turned freelance operative – working for the arms dealers and some terrorist assholes. It's not until 17 minutes into the movie that I realized its full title is *The Foreigner 2: Black Dawn*. It's actually a sequel to *The Foreigner* from 2003. It feels weird to be writing an essay on a sequel to a movie I didn't see, but I sure as shit ain't going back to watch that first.

…

Okay, fine. I'll go watch *The Foreigner* first.

The Foreigner is a serviceable political action thriller with decent production values. Seagal's "Cold" is doing his standard schtick as a government spook taking on a mission to deliver a mysterious package to his French boss. He's apparently betrayed and must go on the run until he figures out why. The best line (referring to the mysterious package, which another tough guy character – and Ray Park lookalike – wants to open) is: "If you touch it again, I will blow your two-inch dick off." Okay, full disclosure: It was the <u>only</u> good line. The best bit of action was Seagal using a fake package to blow up his would-be killer in a toilet. I'm guessing the explosion ignited all the methane in the shitter, because it took the whole building with it.

The movie eventually trailed off into a boring, convoluted mess. Not-Ray-Park was like Pyper-Ferguson's "Pete Hutter" from *Brisco County Jr.*, in that every time you thought he was dead, he came back for more, spouting off one-liners and bristling with menace. Honestly, Not-Ray-Park was more interesting than Seagal…not that that's a hard thing to accomplish. (Sorry, now I have John Pyper-Ferguson on the brain. But when <u>don't</u> I think about Pete and his piece?)

Back to *Black Dawn*, this flick is a pretty predictable mishmash of action and intrigue. The best thing about the flick is Seagal using a body double for nearly all of the action scenes. Either that, or appearing in some scenes with a terrible, obviously computer-generated backdrops. I chalk it up to Seagal being a completely unathletic and out-of-shape lump at this point in his career (a condition which has only worsened). The second-best thing about the movie is the aforementioned John Pyper-Ferguson. His batshit crazy arms dealer is just as good as the rest of the characters he's portrayed, and far more interesting than Seagal's "Cold". Look, I'm sorry I'm talking about John Pyper-Ferguson so much. He's just a great actor, and far too good to be in this kind of low-rent garbage.

We all know Seagal. We've heard all the stories: He shit himself when Gene LeBell put him in a headlock. He slammed John Leguizamo into a wall. He lied about being in the CIA, studying in Japan, and a myriad of other things. He runs like a girl. We all <u>know</u>.

But who we <u>should</u> be talking about is John Pyper-Ferguson. His delightfully zany (and seemingly unkillable) Pete Hutter on *Brisco County, Jr.*, mastermind Stanton Parrish on *Alphas*, and guest-starring roles on pretty much every TV series you've ever (and never) heard of. <u>And</u> a lot of big screen and small screen flicks. I mean, look at this list: *Prom Night II, Bird on a Wire,* Clint Eastwood's *Unforgiven, Pearl Harbor, X-Men: The Last Stand, Drive, Wolves, MacGyver, Star Trek: The Next Generation, Walker, Texas Ranger, Highlander, Vanishing Son, Legend, Lonesome Dove, The X-Files, Nash Bridges, The Outer Limits, Millennium, The Warlord: Battle for the Galaxy, The Crow: Stairway to Heaven, Harsh Realm, Arli$$, ER, CSI: Crime Scene Investigation, 24, Smallville, The Closer, Battlestar Galactica, The L Word, Bones, Criminal Minds, Lost, White Collar, Castle, Fringe, Grimm, Longmire, Once Upon a Time, Burn Notice, The Last Ship, Suits, American Horror Story, Agents of S.H.I.E.L.D., The 100,* and *The Blacklist.* Some of those shows, he was on in multiple roles in multiple episodes…and he's only 56! Imagine what a star he could be with the right role and some attention. What is Seagal in the face of such greatness? We should be doing a book of essays about this guy, instead of a fat, washed-up action "star".

No, I'm not bitter. At all.

I made this essay <u>exactly</u> 1,000 words. Not because I <u>had</u> to, but because I <u>wanted</u> to. Plus, I haven't written a lot of essays before, so I really wanted to see if I could push the envelope and get it done. I proved something to myself today. And that's really the name of the game here. <u>Not</u> talking about Steven Seagal. I just enjoy challenges.

Anyway, *Black Dawn* is a fine diversion, if you're not too picky. Only watch it if you have a few hours (and some brain cells) to kill. I doubt it's the worst of Seagal's oeuvre, but it's way down the list from his best. But let's be honest: Everything he's done except for a few flicks at the start of his career are pretty much at the bottom of the list, amirite?

–Kurt Belcher

"Lightning Bolt Energy Drink" (2006)

Once Red Bull hit shelves promising to give you wings, hundreds of energy drink brands appeared to give you the same kind of boost laced with the same kind of horrendous aftertaste. Not to be outdone, the ponytailed wonder himself jumped in with two horrid flavors under the label Lightning Bolt. I could spend time describing the cough syrup-like palate jackhammering tongue battery of Cherry Charge or Asian Experience, whatever the hell that's supposed to mean. I did try both. I did regret each purchase. That would be pointless, though, considering the fact that these haven't been produced in many years. Plus, if you really want the experience, Asian or otherwise, just grab one of the bizarre off brands you find at a dollar store or the back wall of a Big Lots for a similar grotesque assault on your taste buds. On top of it all, this book is *Hard to Watch*, not *Hard to Drink*, so I want to take a different angle.

Seagal filmed what feels like a mini-infomercial for his liquid slop. It is, like his movies of that time period and beyond, best left to late night YouTube curiosity. It's seemingly narrated by me doing my Jason Statham impression, and opens to a young woman filling a pool with Lightning Bolt, because Stevie wanted to swim in it with her. After she proclaims that she only has two thousand cans left to open, they tell each other how much they love one another before he shoves her back into the pool. Then, in a moment that would be considered ahead of its time on certain adult film sites today, her sister brings him a tray of food before kissing him and jumping in. Good news, everyone! This exact situation could be your life if you drink Lightning Bolt. Steven Seagal says so.

There is a silver lining to all of this. The homemade commercials available can be a lot more fun than the original. In one, a man named Wes drinks a can and immediately becomes Seagal. He then walks through the streets of Toronto ripping limbs off of everyone he meets. In another, a school video project shows Seagal appearing in a Lightning Bolt to a kid who was bullied. He then chugs what's actually a Monster to become strong. Still better production value than the real commercial. TastesLikeTV.com ponders how Seagal discovered the secret of the Lightning Bolt in a documentary style short that's worth a watch. In one scene, Seagal battles several men with one finger. A second part to this saga is promised, but much like Seagal himself, they never deliver.

If you've never had Lightning Bolt, don't fret. Asia still exists, so you're free to experience it on your own. Also, nature still makes cherries and lightning, so enjoy. Consider yourself lucky to know it only as a legend. One day, our grandchildren will speak of this as a fable we told them while we were drunk and filling our bathtubs with Powerade Zero. It's good to be the king.

–Kevin Moyers

Mercenary for Justice (2006)

I watch every mercenary movie I can find. Doesn't matter how cheesy or preposterous. I think my fascination with them started with *The Dogs of War*. Seeing that film as a kid, it just triggered something primal in me.

As an actor, playing a mercenary is a dream role. You can be the ultimate villain and madman and action hero all rolled up in one. Don't forget a brooding reject of society who longs for adventure in distant lands. Or some rebel without a cause, except collecting a paycheck in his own stylish uniform. There's so much you can do with a mercenary character. Mercs were made to be in the movies.

Watching Christopher Walken in *The Dogs of War* really had a big influence on me becoming an actor. His performance, and that movie in general set me on a course of devouring any hired gun movie I could find. Sadly, though, it's been mostly downhill since watching that great movie all those years ago. As much as I adore them, collect them, fawn over them... none of these merc films seem to have the juice that *The Dogs of War* had. Even the movies with far bigger budgets and the latest dazzling technology and effects.

It's not that the movie industry is afraid of making them. Quite the contrary, Hollywood is constantly producing these films and spending fortunes on them. But, for whatever reason, it's just not attracting that visionary filmmaker or that right set of producers who want to make the *Raiders of the Lost Ark* of mercenary films.

Yes, you can always get your kicks, forgive the pun, with one of those rock 'em, sock 'em Jason Statham movies on cable. Or the gimmicky *Expendables* Stallone franchise (best viewed with equally gimmicky flavored whiskeys). Or Dolph Lungren hired to battle an army of infected hordes following a viral outbreak (timely!). Or Brigitte Nielson leading an all-female merc squad (you missed that one?). Yes, there are plenty to go around, year after year, with a feast of firepower and glitz... and plenty of cheese.

It just seems that these soldier of fortune movies are not taking themselves too seriously. They're product. Put in the bankable genre stars, the blood and guts action, and, oh yeah, don't forget the meager, throw away plot. Next, add plenty of hot chicks and sprinkle in a few cameos with some MMA guys. Then dowse the movie with tons of explosions, cool guns and sleek helicopters. Wrap it all up, put an ISBN number on it and send it out to market. And don't put anything in that's too cerebral or profound. That could spoil the whole thing.

Admittedly, that formula usually works. I always go see them at theaters or buy them online. People the world over do the same, too.

But it remains perplexing why this sub-genre of contracted killer movies has not evolved to a higher level of sophistication. Ironically, horror movies have shown up more of late at the Academy Awards and are talked highly about in film and even academic circles. Another competing sub-genre like post-apocalyptic sci fi has produced far more thought-provoking movies like *The Book of Eli* and *Children of Men*, consistently wrangling in way more A-list celebs.

These soldier of fortune movies remain the ugly duckling of genre films. Not really worth too much conversation, even when they do great box office. They're a guilty pleasure, and then quickly forgotten about. Purely escapist fun, mostly disposable, and certainly not to be taken seriously at all. The bourgy film crowd around town doesn't even take the time to trash them.

Which brings us, finally, to the subject of this essay: Steven Seagal's *Mercenary for Justice*. Well, it immediately stumbled right off the bat, spelling Ops wrong at the very beginning of the movie. They spelled it with two p's. 'Opps.' Oops! What a goof.

As I settled into the movie, though, you can't deny its robust production value, gorgeous cinematography and great locations. You gotta' give the movie credit for that. I was really getting hopeful that this movie would surprise me, as movies sometimes do.

But... I just couldn't follow the plot. I have no idea, really, what the movie is about. Someone important got kidnapped and then everybody started shooting everybody. They all eventually made their way to a prison, and then a bank vault. Many things got blown up.

According to Wikipedia, the poor director had to deal with a butchered and nonsensical script abandoned by a series of writers, and producers who were consumed by the war they were waging against... get this... Steven Seagal. What a surprise.

But hey, the more I was watching the movie, the more I was enjoying it. Lots of great action and stunts. Even the terrible script was pretty funny. I think I laughed at all of Steven Seagal's inane one-liners. And who could forget the gorgeous bad-ass merc chick in the black tank top beating up all the French commandos? And the fluorescent orange tank that got blown up? Fluorescent orange! Aren't tanks *not* supposed to stand out in terrain? This was as cheesy and whacky as it gets, and I was eating it all up.

So, the film turned out to be, well... I hope the publisher of this book forgives me... *easy to watch*. Who am I, after all, to judge any of these films? I've been in movies where the budget was probably the cost of the coffee budget for one day on *Mercenary for Justice*. I'm sure if I got cast in that movie, ol' Steven wouldn't have run lines with me or given me the time of day. But, man... it sure would've been fun to be on that crazy set.

Anyone know if he's casting for his next movie?

–Jed Rowen

Shadow Man (2006)

In a conversation with my brother recently I concluded that we are the perfect audience for movies. We enjoy movies quite a bit, be they cinematic classics or b-movie schlock. Whether it be *Citizen Kane* or *Attack of the Mushroom People,* we simply love movies and we've become adept at turning off our brains, suspending disbelief and totally losing ourselves in a movie no matter the quality.

Mind you, this does not make us immune to bad movies. There's a level of terrible that a movie can reach where it becomes impossible to enjoy. I'm sad to say that I reached this point with the second Steven Segal film I was asked to review for this record, 2006's *Shadow Man.* You see, for me to get into a movie to a point where I actually enjoy, I need the bare minimum of a comprehensible story with characters that I can at least try to care about. This movie did not meet those minimum requirements.

The story is unimportant. Segal plays a guy named "Jack" something or other. His wife is dead, and his daughter is a bad actress. At some point she's kidnapped, and he's betrayed by someone who I think is his old friend to the. . .mob? Terrorists? Rogue CIA agents? I don't even know; they might as well have just been wearing T-shirts that said "Bad Guy" on them. Honestly the story of this film is so in memorable it's virtually an anti-meme. It slips out of your mind when you're trying to recall it, your brain unable to accept that something so utterly uninteresting could exist.

I think my biggest problem in this movie isn't the shoddy film making, I can deal with bad directing and bad special effects, it's just an air of rampant laziness that infects the whole production. It feels like somebody fed every scene into a freeware movie editor and chopped it up in an afternoon. The music is generic and uninteresting, the action is slow and boring and literally no one involved with the movie seemed to be putting in anything but a minimal effort. It's as if the producers of this movie got bored with it halfway through and gave up.

In the case of Segal himself he seems to be putting in even less than the minimum. Most scenes of Segal's character that don't directly show his face is an obvious stand-in as whoever they got looked like they were 50 pounds lighter than the rather portly Segal, and apparently a brunette under the ponytail wig the poor guy had to wear. The action scenes to be happening *around* Segal, with him occasionally waving an arm, raising a gun or walking briskly while stuntmen and sound effects fill in the rest. The most Segal did was give a half-hearted lesson in Dim-Mok at the beginning of the film that looks like it was clipped out of a different movie an included the deliciously absurd line "Sifu, teach me how you destroyed the watermelon," which was inadvertently the funniest line of the movie.

I think the best way to describe the action of this movie is as follows: An overweight, middle-aged, tired looking Steven Segal waving his arms around half-heartedly while a group of people with far more talent than he tries to make audiences mistake what they are watching for an action scene. Those poor stuntmen, heading off to Hollywood with a head full of dreams and a heart full of hope. They were probably so happy when they heard they'd be working with Steven Segal, thinking it's their big break only to have Segal put in so little effort I think the fight scenes would have turned out more exiting if he took a nap.

So, while I'm prepared to face down bad movies like *Yor: The Hunter From the Future Battle Beyond the Stars*, and *Machine Girl*, I wasn't prepared for *Shadow Man*. You see even cheesy, badly put together movies had people putting their all into it. Ed Wood did 10-hour days on *Bride of the Monster* and had some illusions about it being a good movie. I can handle bad filmmaking, at least that's fun. *Shadow Man* has no passion behind it, no love, no interest from the filmmakers. Everyone involved seemed to be waiting for their paycheck to clear without much interest in how the film played out.

As for the part of the man himself… as previously mentioned, Sensei Segal is barely there. In my previous review I talk about how Segal used to be everyone's hero, how we all wanted to be like him. In this movie I don't even think Segal wants to be Segal. He doesn't come off as a badass man on a mission, at best I would call him "Grumpy." Gone is the flare of energy and cock-sure bravado that young Segal had, left us a man whose laziness knows no bounds. I guess some men age like fine wine, getting sweeter with every passing year, and other men age like milk, sour and bitter.

–Joshua Knode

Attack Force (2006)

As a youth, in the early 90's nothing got this movie nerd going more than a balls-to-the-wall, testosterone-fueled action flick starring the usual suspects: Arnold Schwarzenegger, Sylvester Stallone, and Chuck Norris. Arnie and Sly were getting too repetitive and Chuck was comfortable being a certain Texas Ranger. Around 1988, the soft-spoken Akido specialist, Steven Seagal came on the scene with two superb cop films, Andrew Davis' *Above the Law* and *Hard to Kill* --starring future wife and frequent speed bag, Kelly LeBrock. Seagal soon climbed his way to the very top of my mantle of badass action heroes. Sadly... he didn't last that long.

So, let's fast-forward about sixteen years - Steven is a now a direct to video darling and looking like a slightly more mobile Marlon Brando, just with black dye in his hair. Seagal is still the aikido master, but he's also incorporated the art of KFC. Michael Keusch's *Attack Force* has Commander Lawson (Seagal) leading a group of young soldiers who are in between some covert gigs. During a night of partying, they become separated after three of these exceptionally horny soldiers come enamored and gorgeous yet ever so mysterious gal in a nightclub. This mysterious gal isn't just your average busty barfly – she's a homicidal vixen and juiced up on a party drug called "CTX." This stuff ain't your grandma's party drug as it enables the user to attain a super human strength. Let's just say that the menage y trois between Commander Lawson's boys and this ferocious female ends with the splattering of the wrong kinds of fluids – the red kind.

What looks like an isolated incident of murder, gradually weaves its way to being something much more sinister - with CTX being a way to create groups of super soldiers to be used for war. Lawson and few reliable allies are thrusted into seeking out the man distributing CTX, a shadowy nightclub regular, Seth (Matthew Chambers). Even with this tall order ahead of him, Lawson needs a time for a lil' sumthin- sumthin. Every hero (even of the morbidly obese variety) needs some time for some loving. Thankfully, this particular scene is clothed and very brief. Yes, the trademark belly-shielding black coat stays on Seagal's three-hundred-pound frame! Whew!!

Attack Force director Michael Keusch had the dubious honor of helming two other Seagal vehicles, *Shadow Man* and *Flight of Fury*. The fact that Seagal and Keusch worked on three movies together must mean they have some chemistry, right? In all honesty, these gentlemen are no Burt Reynolds and Hal Needham in this particular collaboration. I have yet to see either of those films but let's just say that the bar is not high. Technically, it's a mess. One glaring issue is the fact that Seagal's voice has been dubbed in several sequences. I'm just guessing here, but it's very possible he was talking so low that his lines weren't audible. Mr. Seagal was probably not down with having to come in for the few minutes of work to fix it in post-production. Instead, what we have is a voice actor doing an impression of Michael Madsen doing Commander Lawson's lines. I will say that this notable flaw is ridiculous but I couldn't help but laugh. Yes, I was entertained, but I've also seen Hudson Hawk seven times.

While the plot of *Attack Force* takes place in Paris, it is actually shot in Romania. It kind of gave off an Eastern Europe vibe early on with so many shots of cobblestone and architecture common in that part of the world. This helps with the visuals and at times pulls you away from some silliness that is on screen during the ninety minute plus running time.

Aside from the dubbing blunder, another interesting tidbit about the film is that it was supposedly going to be a vampire film almost in the Underworld ilk. From watching the film you can definitely see the possibility of this change in the script, as our CTX addicts could very easily have been a group of powerful bloodsuckers. Rumor has it that Russian president Vladimir Putin has an uncut three hundred minute 3-D version of this masterwork. Okay, I kid. It's not in 3D.

The action scenes in *Attack Force* are pretty solid. One thing I was amazed to see is the usage of practical effects and actual blood squibs during the shoot-outs. You kind of almost expect with this movie being on the lower budget side that the producers would get lazy in that regard and we'd be inundated with CGI to save a few bucks. If you like gore you'll be pleased to see plenty of arteries gushing, in addition to the splashy shoot-outs. Sadly, the great action scenes don't involve our star. Seagal's signature bone-breaking from his earlier classics is nowhere to be found in this offering. However, breadsticks at Olive Garden are an achievable feat for the six-foot-four action movie legend. The handful of action scenes that Seagal participates in are pretty difficult to digest as they don't have the devastating appeal of his sensational early years. This 2006 version of Seagal paws in the air like an excited feline who just got one of those shitty *Dollar Store* mouse-on-a-rope toys. At one point I are started to chuck *Meow Mix* at the screen until he finally stopped. He finally did, I rubbed his belly, and we both passed out.

Going into *Attack Force*, I was quite nervous as to whether I would be able to finish the film. It took a couple of days and several libations, but I pushed through and actually enjoyed portions of the film. There are certainly worse films in this that are being in this book. The pacing and generous action throughout keeps *Attack Force* from falling into the heap Seagal dreck. If you have a hankering for a unique, ultra-violent and reasonably fun low-budget action film then *Attack Force* could be your cup of Udon.

–Jeff Dolniak

Flight of Fury (2007)

The X-77 is a stealth bomber that has technology that scares the shit even out of us, as General Barnes (Angus MacInnes, or Gold Leader – *for those who know*) boldly declares before the one man he knows who can bring his $75 million dollar piece of military hardware back in one piece. That man is Steven Seagal, still with a little moxie on his side, as John Sands. He's a hero that was apparently sent to prison for a stupid reason, and though the General doesn't blame him for doing what he did (*we never find out what that is*), he had to have his mind wiped because John knows a lot of things that make a lot of people nervous.

This offer is presented to Seagal only after he escapes from prison, steals a car and reveals himself to the authorities by stopping a little highway robbery. The mind wipe Sands/Seagal endured did little to affect his skills as the greatest stealth pilot on the planet, and the teacher of rogue aviator Ratcher (Steve Toussaint, *Prince of Persia: The Sands of Time*) who has stolen the Air Force's prize bird.

Fury unfolds as the Kmart amalgamation of *Broken Arrow* mixed with *The Rock*, minus the Bayhem and the John Woo cool. Seagal like Connery in *The Rock* teams up with a young hotshot named Jannick (Mark Bazeley, *The Bourne Ultimatum*), who, while being drinkin' age, according to Seagal, "isn't combat ready." Still, the man is under orders, so they come up with a daring plan to find this plane, which is the 2007 cheap effects equivalent of Wonder Woman's invisible jet.

The boys are to land, find the plane and fly it out...or blow it up if shit gets too real. So they hop over to Northern Afghanistan to the secret headquarters of the Black Sunday Terrorist Group led by Stone (Vincenzo Nicoli, *The Dark Knight*) and his spicy warrior woman Eliana (Kati Jones, *Mistresses*), the only cats for miles with British accents. With the stolen jet Stone plans to fire missiles that contain a deadly toxin that could kill all of us in 48 hours. Sands and Jannick are separated; Jannick is tortured as Sands goes in search of his "still fine as Hell" asset in the form of Jessica (Ciera Payton, *The Runner*), who brings a nice lesbian seduction as distraction scene to aid Sands in his infiltration.

But the boys have been out of contact for more than 22 hours and the General is feeling that icy chill run up his spine, so he calls his buddy Admiral Frank Pendleton (Tim Woodward, *The Scarlet Letter*), and tells him he'll buy him a goddamn case of scotch, single malt, if his fleet would alter their course to provide air cover for the secret operation. The General and his XO, Commander Bud Jackson (Gary Cooper – *not that one, the other*), whom he lovingly refers to as Bud in different exchanges, has a problem with all the secrecy, yet when push comes to shove he is happy to join his commanding officer in throwing the damn rule book out and kickin' some ass. Thus the plan becomes simple. If Sands cannot escape with the jet or blow it all sky high, then Navy pilots will swarm in and dust the bastards down.

Sands and Jessica team up with Rojar (Alki David, *The Bank Job*), and together they scratch out a plan for storming the castle, taking on 60 heavily-armed multi-national mercenaries, without guns, only knives…'cause they know how to use knives. From here the film actually picks up a pulse as the action is fluent and each character gets a fight sequence. Seagal, who was clearly on the film for a designated period of time to complete all his shots, spends the opening of the battle sitting there with a remote control and just blows shit up? Jessica and Eliana manage a brief girl fight over the sides that they serve and the bitterness of one side feeling slighted after leaving their last encounter so unsatisfied.

Seagal finally pops up in the hanger, frees Jannick who goes after Ratcher who double-crosses Stone because America is all about makin' money, and he's all about bein' shown *all the money*! Seagal shows us he does know how to use a knife, and with Navy planes inbound Sands and Jessica take off in the X-77 convenient leaving Jannick to be killed by Ratcher who takes off in another jet to get into a little fancy dancin' in a roughly 8-minute dogfight in which Seagal shows us the X-77's awesome cloaking ability for as long as the budget allows. "I could out fly you in a school bus," Ratcher blurts with steely bravado as the pupil and the master take center stage, exchange a few dramatic looks into camera, shoot at eat other with what could be stock footage till, at last, Sands shows the young gun that he ain't done being top gun by blowing him to kingdom come.

Yes, it took old John a while, he had to jumpstart his camel...and he's carrying hazardous material on his plane, yet the mission is complete. Sands and the General meet again as friends. Seagal doesn't have to salute him anymore, 'cause he's not in the military, but the General won't miss the salute as much as he'll miss the man who was jailed for knowing too much, who regrettably left a good man to die, even though he secretly thought he was an asshole. Seagal teamed with collaborators Michael Keusch (*Attack Force, Shadow Man*) and Joe Haplin (*Attack Force, Shadow Man*) in this, yet another entry in the stealth mission that was the latter day Seagal's flight from cinematic relevance. He saw himself still as the hero in the white hat, hiding that hair now dyed jet-black to hide the fact...that old gray mare, ain't who he used to be.

–Kent Hill

Urban Justice (2007)

The first thing I noticed about *Urban Justice* is that it's actually called *Renegade Justice*. Why the producers felt the need to make that change isn't clear, but after an opening that looks and sounds like a dumbed down Hallmark film, we are treated to a scene in the city, AKA the *urban* area in question, and the aggressively generic hip hop music signifies the area as dangerous. So it's no surprise when a photographer that we've been watching since the beginning of the film IMMEDIATELY stumbles onto some kind of *renegade* drug deal and snaps several incriminating pics, thereby insuring that the next scene in the film will be his brutal demise.

At nearly 7 minutes, we FINALLY get to the moment we've been so desperately waiting for...the triumphant entrance of one Mr. Steven Seagal, shown in an excruciatingly tight closeup. Our hero resembles a cross between Vegas era Elvis and a pained Johnny Galecki, grimacing as if he's just been taken to task by an angry Darlene Conner (or gobbled down a particularly heavy fried peanut butter and banana sandwich just prior to his arrival).

It quickly becomes clear (sort of) that Simon (Seagal's character) has a history of some sort with the photog in question, because he does that old "I'll stand 100 feet away from the funeral in a weird conspicuous attempt at being inconspicuous" thing. The next scene takes us to a different, equally offensive, generic hip hop song as Simon drives through the *urban* neighborhood in search of "random gang members"...and we are off and running!

As Simon rents an uproariously amusing messy room (complete with an empty water bottle tipped over on a table and one single shirt hanging from a drawer), the script helpfully guides us into discovering that the photographer was a cop...and he was Simon's son!

Two gang members threaten Simon for no given reason, and he is forced to handle them as quickly and violently as possible, with some funny cuts highlighting the *urban* skirmish. But nothing can prepare us For Seagal's amazing, super-*urban* delivery of the snort inducing line, "Tell every muthafucka on the street they not safe 'til I find the mothafucka who killed my son."

It is at this moment that Simon has touched our souls and perhaps Seagal has taken his first step toward that elusive Oscar nomination.

Several bizarre transitions and yet another incredibly generic hip hop song later, and Simon has adapted his "I'm relating to urbanized characters accent" once again. He gonna find his son's killer, yo. You muthafucka.

DRINKING GAME: take a shot whenever Simon spits out the phrase "muthafucka that killed my son." Then prepare not to drive until the next day.

When you need a super evil, ultra-*urban* bad guy, who else can you turn to but the sinister, scare inducing Eddie Griffin. He does his best to put us in the mind of Wesley Snipes or Ice Cube. He comes off more like an agitated Eddie Griffin, but it's a valiant effort that deserves to be noted (I suppose).

35 minutes or so in, we are finally treated to another familiar face, Machete himself: Danny Trejo. Trejo is (regrettably for him, one assumes) a boss level character named El Chivo. Trejo does provide the first natural sounding use of the word "motherfucker" in the entire film. The likable, omnipresent Trejo delivers lines with the same verve that he would in a better film, and as we watch Seagal try to recite his detached volleying dialogue to Trejo, we are wishing we WERE watching one of those better films...*Sin City*, or Rob Zombie's *Halloween*, or even *Storks*. But naw, here we are in Steven Seagal world, desperate for another generic rap song signifying a merciful credits crawl.

It's not that *Urban Justice* or *Renegade Justice* or whatever the hell it's called is a BAD film...well, yeah it is. But it's also a sad, hilarious, completely cynical film full of clichés, stereotypes, and dozens of macho types saying the word "motherfucker" with varying degrees of threatening success. This is the kind of movie where we know that some kind of plot or plan is supposed to be happening by the sound of the "eighties heist movie" music, but who the hell knows what it is?

A few notes...the polished stock footage used for establishing shots is absolutely jarring by contrast to the way the rest of the flick looks. And why the hell is LITERALLY every scene with a gun filmed in slow motion?

DRINKING GAME #2: Take a drink every time you see a slow-motion shootout. And then go directly to bed, if you can make it all the way to your bed.

Hilariously, for some weird urban, somewhat renegade-ass reason, the ending of the film eludes to an East coast/West coast rivalry.

My wife declined to enjoy this film with me, but she did ask me quizzically, "Can Steven Seagal actually act?" And that is a more complicated question than I had originally considered. The short answer is probably, "Ehhhh...", but I will say this...he really plays this character. And he has played this character a lot. Like, a lot. Generally, we get more hints of his backstory than we do here in this picture, but it's still pretty much the same dude. He has a dwindling modicum of charisma and a little bit of presence. As a kid I watched his films with glee and I wanted to be like him, back when he could lift his leg a little bit higher and didn't need the camera angles to make him look ferocious. Which is ok, even for an urban pile of renegade like this...he's older and it happens. He can still get the job done in his way.

But I didn't want to be in this movie, and from the looks of things, neither did he.

–Paul Counelis

Pistol Whipped (2008)

In *Pistol Whipped*, Steven Seagal plays Matt, an ex-special forces person/cop turned Alcoholic Gambling Divorcee who owes money all over town and is a deadbeat father to his daughter. When all of Matt's markers which come to over a million dollars that are bought by the mysterious Old Man (yes, that is his character name) played by Lance Henriksen and with the assistance of his Henchman Blue played by *Pulp Fiction's* Paul Calderon, Matt must assassinate various bad guys the first one is Arthur J. Nascarella's sleazy mobster Bruno who show off how much of an asshole he is by racially insulting an Asian Fruit & Veg woman in his introduction scene.

There's a funny moment for me during this scene Matt walks up to the stall asks her if she speaks Japanese or Korean? she says both Seagal says "me too" and you'd think he would talk to her in either of those languages, but he doesn't the film just cuts away to him stalking the rooftops like tubby, ponytailed Batman.

After the mobsters take down this sets the wheels in motion that may have connections to his former line of work & closer to home involving the good guy partner of his ex-wife played by Blanchard Ryan.

The movie opens with a black & white slow motion shoot out in a graveyard with corrupt cops we find out later in the film wouldn't look out of place in a John Woo movie, although the shards of the obvious foam headstones bouncing near Seagal does make me chuckle. *Pistol Whipped* was written by Ronin Screenwriter

J.D. Zeik gives Seagal a flawed man who is seeking redemption for his sins in church for the sake of his daughter and the leading actor actually shows up giving the most interesting performance during this period of his DTV career. No poorly-dubbed acting or multiple uses of stand-ins in this flick even if the whole plot doesn't make much sense, it's just connective tissue to take us to another shootout.

The action sequences are executed well. With Reine we get Seagal in all his flappy-hand glory, car chases that thrill even with their less-than-stellar driving inserts, and an end shootout which is the highlight of the film for me.

Pistol Whipped was shot in Connecticut choosing not to film in Canada or redressed Eastern European movie backlot, the film has pretty grimy cityscapes mixed with suburban locations using filters to show their contrasts. The camera work by Roel Reine makes this movie stand out in this period of Seagal's career; with many of these movies in the 2000s their cinematography was very tele-visual, but Reine employs handheld and crane work.

The supporting cast features acting great Lance Henriksen as The Old Man who only has a few scenes in the movie that are mostly exposition dumps. His presence is welcome though, since he has worked in everything from Sidney Lumet's *Dog Day Afternoon* to *Alien* then onto multiple straight to DVD sequels in *The Pumpkinhead* franchise with a career still going strong at 80 years old.

Alongside Lance is Paul Calderon's henchman, Blue. Another great actor that first piqued my interest in him when I saw him in the early 90s working with Abel Ferrara for the first time on *King Of New York* and is great as a Professor in Ferrara's black & white vampire flick, *The Addiction* with the rest of his career littered with small roles in big movies plus numerous guest spots in episodic television. During the early 90s he auditioned for a role in Quentin Tarantino's *Pulp Fiction,* coming very close to being cast in the Jules Winfield role. In *Pistol Whipped*, Calderon pulls the strings with the Matt character, trading bullets with the bad guys in the final climax.

It's also amazing to see former Captain America Matt Salinger, son of the *Catcher in the Rye* author, J.D., in a blink and you'll miss it role-playing a card dealer during the film's title sequence as Seagal's character is having a bad gambling night.

There is a romantic subplot with Matt and Drea, played by Renee Elise Goldsberry, who can be seen in the recent production of monster hit musical *Hamilton*. The post-coital banter over eggs would make you bring up your breakfast if you sat at the same table hearing them talking about Sensei Seagal's genital size. The DVD does have a small extended sequence of their potential relationship that was cut from the final film and an original ending in which Matt gets his daughter a dog with his ex-wife that hints at a possible reconciliation in their relationship.

The strongest female relationship that Seagal has in the relationship isn't with his bland blonde bimbette ex-wife, though, it is with his daughter Becky, played by Lydia Jordan. The young woman is concerned for her daddy and the lead works well with the young girl in a rare moment of on-screen chemistry.

I do remember seeing *Pistol Whipped* on its initial home rental release in 2008 and it was fine, if a little underwhelming. My feelings haven't changed in the 12 years since. Revisiting it again for this piece in an era that produced some truly unwatchable Steven Seagal movies it stands out, serving more as an introduction to the director's work. Roel Reine would from this go onto become a director-for-hire on low budget sequels to hit franchises that Universal Studios had in their back catalogue working *Death Race 2* and *3* plus follows up to *The Scorpion King* series that would turn a profit in the home video market leading to recent gigs on the American TV series *Black Sails, Blood Drive,* and *Inhumans*.

–Aaron Carruthers

The Onion Movie (2008)

Above the Law

Hard to Kill

Out for Justice

Cock Puncher

Maybe you are not familiar with that last film, but you should be. It just might be the best film in Seagal's ridiculously long career. It has everything a viewer could want from a Seagal movie: the lead character (another actor portraying a young Steven) losing his first battle. Seagal's character asking to be trained by a wise Sensei. A training montage. Overblown, over the top action sequences.

Best of all?

It doesn't really exist.

Cock Puncher is the creation of the fine people from The Onion. The trailer for the fictional film appears in *The Onion Movie* (2008), a series of interconnected sketches revolving around the conflict between a seasoned journalist who believes the focus of the news should be the reporting of actual facts and the sleazy corporate owners who want to commodify the nightly news. Yes, an important topic and one which still resonates today.

However, there is no time for that, we need to talk about the brilliant martial arts techniques of a master whose fighting style is based solely on testicular assault.

Cock Puncher, in the realm of The Onion, is a film due to be released by Global Tetrahedron Pictures. The commercial for the film appears numerous times throughout the film, although the full "trailer" is only shown once.

It is one minute and eighteen seconds of pure joy.

"In a world without justice. Where the strong prey on the weak."

The Seagal stand-in, a thinner, younger, white male with the featured slick back hair that was the staple of pre-ponytail Seagal. It's the look he sported when he was till claiming to have Italian heritage and ties to organized crime. Unfortunately, it is this version of the Cock Puncher who takes all of the initial nut-shots. We see him attacked by a gang of generic oriental thugs who beat him mercilessly, one punch to the groin after another.

The same character then begs his teacher to train him in this esoteric art. He claims that he is ready but is proven wrong when the Sensei punches him...in the nuts.

This is a rare moment of self-parody for someone who has a history of taking himself way too seriously. Perhaps this is why he is not seen on the receiving end of the titular cock punches. That would be too far for the man who has done everything, according to him, from defeating the Yakuza, to training CIA agents, training multiple UFC champions, and even training under legendary Aikido founder Morihei Ueshiba (which would have been done at age 13 if one does the math). Why then, would he allow himself to be satirized in this fashion?

Easy answer, as hinted above, he really isn't. We never see Seagal losing, or even taking a punch in the *Cock Puncher* trailer. Instead, we see his name announced in an explosion. He (by which we mean his double) rides into the scene on a motorcycle, wearing a yellow kimono which instantly calls to mind the famous track suit worn by Bruce Lee in *Game of Death* except with red accents instead of black. He takes out two guards at once, then faces off against a circle of ninjas -- in slow motion! This is Seagal in all of his bombastic glory.

What cinches it, however, is the end of the film. Without going into a ridiculous amount of detail regarding the plot, the climax of the film takes place in The Onion Newsroom. Anchorman Norm Archer, the reporter who has been fighting against the corporate types, is interrupted by terrorists who take over the newsroom. All looks lost until the arrival of...

...Cock Puncher.

One should note that this type of crossing between the fictional world of the film itself and the "reality" of the Onion universe happens continuously. In this world it makes sense that the fictional character whose film has been advertised on this television station would also be a person (whose only name is the name of his fictional character) who could then stride into the newsroom. And stride he does. Cock Puncher takes out a number of black robed terrorists armed with scimitars. Before he can take on the terrorists, they reveal their ultimate weapon.

They have land mines strapped over their groins, totally negating the Cock Puncher's ability to punch cocks. A Britney Spears surrogate named Melissa Cherry attempts to "distract" the terrorists, but it is ultimately Peruvians with laser eyes (just go with it) who are able to defeat the land mine, allowing Cock Puncher to perform a flying cock punch. The other terrorist surrenders, not because of being outnumbered, not because of the loss of his comrades, but because of the rousing speech given by Seagal's character and the fact that he loves the action hero.

There were rumors of a full=length comedy spoofing action movies that would have starred Seagal, but the film never came to fruition. One doubts that such a movie would have been approved by the action star, as it would have actually spoofed the characters that appear so central to his sense of self-identity. How could someone who has come to view himself as a champion of law and justice stoop so low as to make fun of these same tropes?

No, the only spoofing one can see is that which happens in *The Onion Movie*. Not a Frank Drebin buffoon who stumbles his way through solving crimes, but a character who is only parody in the sense of being an aggrandized version of his characters, and one suspects, himself.

Make fun of Seagal? As Cock Puncher would answer, "I don't think you've got the balls."

–Michael Cieslak

Kill Switch (2008)

If you look up best Steven Seagal movies on Google, you get a film named *Kill Switch* from 2008. It took $10,000,000 to make but went straight to DVD and $5.99. Watching this film, I wonder how it even made the list. How bad were the other ones that didn't make it? It is still a Seagal film. Same man, same haircut, same look on his face like he is trying to pass a turd sideways. You know it is a Seagal film because right when it starts, his name is HUGE on the screen in case you forget. The only other name mentioned: Issac Hayes in small font at the bottom. I will be talking about four things: Seagal's character, action, cast and the story itself.

Stevie plays a "not-by-the-book" cop with a dramatic past named Jacob King. Of course, he has the word "king" in his name. When he was younger, his twin brother was murdered. 85 years later and now he is a cop in Memphis, Tennessee. The first five words out of his mouth have a nice Southern twang. The next sentence it transforms into a ghetto Southern offspring. There are black people in the film and Seagal talks in the most horrible slang towards them. He calls everyone "baby" and when things get bad uses, "lord all mighty." His dialogue is filled with multiple bad puns that you can look up on any "pun of the day" website. The best line he has was, "I will shove my size 14 shoe up your ass." I mean, at least we know his shoe size now. The more I watched him, the more I thought this was a joke. He would have many serious scenes, but with that accent, you couldn't help but laugh. The Sensei Seagal serious factor is just zero with that accent.

After a flashback, the movie starts with action. It consists of Seagal throwing a character named Billy Joe into the wall twenty times. There are a few fight scenes throughout this film and Seagal just looks tired. He uses a stunt double, as per usual, and the double took hits, threw punches, jumped, walked, stood still, hailed a cab. They couldn't have picked a worse double, too. If you think Seagal's hair looks painted on and fake, you should have seen the wig for the stunt double. I could buy a better one at Walmart on a Wednesday night 'cause it's weird there. The stunt double had the build of a young Seagal and the face of Danny Trejo. You know, the guy from *Machete*. All they did for these scenes was film Seagal moving from side to side and then would splice in the punches, just like a 12-year-old editing his first YouTtube video. Besides his fists Seagal had another weapon of choice: a magical handgun. Why is it magical? Well, it can shoot over 100 rounds without reloading. It can make things like a car, or a large pipe explode. There is a downside. A "price" for that magic. You need to fire it 100 times before you can hit your target. That's right, worse than a storm trooper shooting Rebel scum. I will say that the last fight scene actually had Seagal move more. He moved some and threw Billy Joe around again. With this stellar review, I bet you want to hear my top three action moments of the movie. There are two because I couldn't think of a third. The top one was the killer beating a hooker to death with a crying baby doll. You want to watch the movie now, don't you? The other one was pimp getting his teeth knocked out on a table. The silver lining.

The venerable IMDb says this is an action, crime, drama, thriller, so it has that going for it. *Kill Switch* teaches you about prostitution, sexism, racism, attempted rape, murder, domestic abuse… it has a real social conscience. For example, it starts off with a flashback of a kid watching his twin brother get murdered. This kid is Seagal, though, and if I knew I was going to grow up to look like him, I would quit life, too. This tortures Seagal's character mind throughout the film. What does this mean? Nothing at all. It has nothing to do with the film. There is a main killer in the film and a side baddie. The baddie is in the beginning and Seagal just doesn't like him. Throughout the film he is trying to catch the main killer, Lazarus. A man, or maybe a special boss in an RPG, he kills women with something to do about the moon cycles and astrological shit… or something. Seagal will explain it for you. He figures it out pretty fast, so don't expect a big reveal. The killer is not really killer-y looking, but he does pull off a nice black thong showing his toned butt cheeks. There are other characters in this film, but they don't really help Seagal, or the story, at all. This was Issacs Hayes' last role and maybe this flick is what killed him. That sad moment aside, most of the film is Seagal trying to catch the killer and he does. Everyone thinks Steve is the killer for about three minutes and then Lazarus confesses to all of it. A twist or lazy writing? You be the judge.

I can't stop without talking about the end of the film. A spoiler, but you need to know. Near the end, the side baddie comes back and kills Seagal's girlfriend. Again, he is so upset. I think I saw a tear, but realized it was that "I just ate a lemon" face. Once Seagal's character is cleared and he is not pinned for the murders, it is already too late; she is gone. Then, the end of the film shows him walking into a huge house. He kisses his white as white can be Russian wife and gives his Russian children, played by local Mexican actors, presents. The children run off with the maid. He then follows his trophy wife upstairs where she pops out her boobs to seduce him. Disclaimer: these are the only live boobs in the film. He ends the film by flashing that sly Seagal smile, looking like face you make when you are mid orgasm and someone walks in on you.

Kill Switch is a horrible film, but it is a must watch for any Steven Seagal fan. Buy it, rent it, or do what I did, watch it free on a streaming service with ads, because that is how great it is.

–Paul Celano

Sounds from the Crystal Cave / Mojo Priest (2008)

Can we call it a sin that so few even know of the musical prowess of one Steven Seagal? I'm about to find out. I will give you a song-by-song rundown of each track off his debut musical effort *Songs from the Crystal Cave*, as well as his other album *Mojo Priest*, which I'm guessing is going to be the more hilarious of the two. But what is the Crystal Cave? I'd like to imagine it's like his fortress of solitude, where the sacred crystals empower his mind and soul to create spiritually elevating and enlightening chords and melodies. Well, I'm about to give both albums an honest listen and find out.

SONGS FROM THE CRYSTAL CAVE

"Girl, it's Alright" – An actual catchy, foot-tapper of a mellow pop song. This actually could have been a bigger hit than it was, and I could easily see it playing in regular rotation on the speakers of corporate grocery store chains. It did see some attention at the time of its release, even an official music video. Maybe this Seagal guy was onto something.

"Don't You Cry" - Hmm. Actually not half bad. Another one I could easily imagine hearing as I walk into a grocery store. Much better than any Collective Soul song I ever heard that was released at the time. Nice use of chord changes. Strong, reassuring lyrics that could easily lift me up in times of sorrow. I mean, what more should I expect from a guy who saves an entire Navy ship from terrorists when he's really just the cook.

"Music" – Okay, he's losing me here. Not catchy. Generic vocals and lyrics. Pass.

"Better Man" – Slow, boring, uninviting acoustic guitar intro. Bored me faster than the last song. Hard pass.

"Route 23" – Okay, not a bad little moody, bluesy guitar intro with some nice licks. Stevie is actually a pretty good blues guitarist I'll give him that. I actually enjoyed this one start to finish. Shows some nice vocal range from our man Steve.

"My God" – Oh shit this one starts out awful. I think he's attempting to rap. It's a little catchy. Lost me at the refrain "My God is better than your God." I'm laughing harder than I did when I saw his sword fight performance in *Machete*.

"Lollipop" – I was expecting a laugh riot from the title. "Lillipop you make my heart go giddy up" followed by some guy spitting reggae rap. This is by far the best and worst track so far.

"Not for Sale" – Yup, Stevie is delving into some world music now. And he should have not. I applaud the ambition, but shit.

"Dance" – He mumbles worse than he does in his normal speech patterns in this one. More world music ambition here. It's like Bollywood Bhangra mixed with Irish fiddle music. I'm regretting taking on this job. Damn you to heck, David Hayes!

"Jealousy" – What the fuck? Pass.

"War" – I think Shakira heard this song as a young girl and said, "I'm gonna this but good."

"Strut" – HOLY FUCKING SHIT. I take it back. This writing assignment was well worth it. THIS IS THE ONLY STEVEN SEGAL SONG THAT MATTERS. He's said the word "punani" like five times already and sang about making a woman come. I had to look up the lyrics. "I WANT THE PUNANI SEE FOR MAKING NICE." Seriously, he's having a back and forth with this female Jamaican singer about coming and punani. Why was this not a hit?

"Goree" – Sorry but I've lost all interest in continuing on with this after hearing "Strut." It's a boring ballad. What more do you need to know?

"The Light" – See above.

MOJO PRIEST

Like I said, after hearing "Strut" and its many lines about making you come and wanting the punani see for making nice, my motivation has waned. But I find myself at more of a loss here than I had expected. I can't really make fun of this. It's really not bad. Sure, it takes itself too seriously, but the same can be said for just about 99% of everyone who has ever picked up a guitar.

It really isn't bad. It's pretty much a straight blues album from start to finish, with hints of traditional country and bluegrass thrown in there. I want to make fun of this, but I seriously can't. Stevie shows us here that he knows his way around a guitar better than he does his way around a movie script. Clocking in at fifty-nine minutes and change, listening to this was far from the worst hour I've spent researching a writing project. I expected to laugh and throw my computer out the window. I actually envisioned myself in a Kentucky blues tavern pounding bourbon and stomping my foot to the beat and really getting into it. Sure, there were a few bricks on here, a seasoned blues fan with no prior knowledge or pop-culture conceptions about the artist might not see any of the irony. I feel like I've failed in my mission here to provide funny commentary on the musical prowess of this guy, but shit, he can sing a blues song and play a twangy six-string pretty damn well. Sorry. It's just the truth.

–Jeff O'Brien

Against the Dark (2009)

So, I asked David Hayes, "What do you need for the book, now it's almost done?" David Hayes, that rat bastard, replied, "I need someone to review *Against the Dark*." And I, inveterate fool that I am, volunteered, "Sure!"

Now, I wasn't expecting much. This is a 2009 Steven Seagal movie. There's as much chance of this not sucking donkey balls as I have of winning the lottery this week and I didn't buy a ticket. But it's also a horror movie, which raised my eyebrows, and I was eager to see how the Rock's cousin and regular stunt double, Tanoai Reed, would manage with second billing. Spoiler: he has little to do and still provides the best scenes.

What I didn't expect was any 2009 movie being *this* bad. It's incoherent, it's contradictory and it's poorly shot, perhaps deliberately. No characters are worthy, no detail is important and no plot is discernible, let alone consistently told. We do know it was made pre-COVID as the infection MacGuffin only spreads because there isn't a vaccine, like that's something people would actually seek out in an apocalypse.

And it has absolutely no idea what it wants to be, though I've finally figured out what I think it is, after watching in increasingly wide-eyed disbelief last night and letting it settle overnight to digest like a bad taco from a Sonoran street cart.

Have you seen the work of the artist who applies professional talent to reimagining children's drawings, preserving their naïveté about how many legs a cat has, which side of its head its eyes are on and whether it's square or triangular? Well, this is precisely that in cinematic form. If a precocious four-year-old boy outlined an action horror movie and industry professionals interpreted his crayon scrawls literally, against their every better judgement, it might play out exactly like *Against the Dark*.

It would star a group of tough guys with ponytails and no expressions and they'd be called Hunters. They'd face the apocalypse in outfits entirely of black leather, like they're working for General Zod. The women have cleavage and high heels. In black leather. They stalk the dimly lit corridors of an abandoned hospital slicing down monsters with their swords because that's what vigilantes sanctioned by the State Department do. None have names but Steven Seagal would be Tao. He'll tell us that fifty minutes in and we won't be sure if we believe him. He's cryptic, muttering things like "We're not here to decide who's right or wrong. We're here to decide who lives or dies."

There would be regular people too whose names you won't ever remember. They're in the hospital too, looking for the exit, though they should have climbed back out of the window they climbed in. Instead, they wander down different corridors in different directions but always end up back together again. A young lady is the leader. The kid might be a boy or a girl. It doesn't matter. They all leave each other behind whenever anything happens, as if they never existed. Maybe they didn't. And whenever things get too bad, the Hunters would be right there to save them. And then leave them behind.

The monsters would be vampires, just because. Except they're not vampires. They're "infected" or "diseased" or "mutants." Not vampires. Maybe that's copyrighted by Disney or something. They hang around this abandoned hospital feeding off people who left when the apocalypse happened but are still there to die on camera whenever there's a need for a gore scene. And there would be lots of gore scenes! We'll know they're gore scenes because they're scenes with gore in them. Oh, and there would be a mad doctor whose daughter is a cool vampire chick. But not the one you think.

The Hunters would take him down in his lab because he's evil even though they don't actually know he exists and neither do we until someone goes to the bathroom. They take down all the monsters with their swords. Slash! Slash! Later, they switch to shotguns for no apparent reason. Boom!

Boom! Every fight scene would happen so quickly that we won't be able to see it, because it'll be shot from the periphery of our vision with rapid fire editing. It's like we'd squeeze our eyes shut when it happens because it's icky, but we'd peek a little too. It's also because Steven Seagal can't move any more, but you're not supposed to know that.

A black dude in a military uniform would be in charge of everything, even the people in charge, like Mr. Cross, who's called that because he's cross with the black dude for approving the sanitising of Sector 7. We won't know what Sector 7 is but it's going to get sanitised. That's all the black dude says, like an action figure who has one line when you pull a string in his back, but he'd be played by someone with immense talent like Keith David, just for a pay check. He'll still approve sanitising Sector 7 even though it contains innocent civilians, but he'll be right because he's in charge.

The end would happen right before the end credits. It'd be full of explosions and bits of buildings flying everywhere, but some of it would be the people driving home and the Hunters walking down a road because the city is safe now, free of any apocalypse in Sector 7 because I have to go to school there tomorrow morning.

And that's how my movie would happen, Daddy! Wouldn't it be great if it could be real? Wouldn't it?

Yeah, it's that bad. To be fair, there are a few moments when characters muse on having become the monsters when the majority are a changed dominant species, but those don't go anywhere. There are good shots of teeth too, whether they're actively being filed or replaced by screws. But that's it. I honestly preferred the IMDb TV ads for bladder control.

–Hal CF Astell

Driven to Kill (2009)

Driven to Kill tells the story of Ruslan, an ex-Russian mobster who retires from fighting, stabbing and killing to become an ace novelist, spinning tales about the good ol' days in the mob. Let's pause there. A novelist? Really?? Seagal's character barely utters coherent sentences when he speaks, I can't imagine what he would be like as a novelist! Sure...whatever. Totally believable. When his daughter Lanie and ex-wife Catherine are viciously attacked on Lanie's wedding day, Ruslan is pulled back into action to seek bloody revenge.

In 2009, Steven Seagal still looked somewhat like Steven Seagal and not the bloated doppelganger he morphed into just a short time later. Not only is Seagal a master of martial arts but in this film he's still very much a master of all 6 or 7 expressions that comprise his spectrum of acting. He uses them all to various degrees of success, from the stoic fifty yard go-to-hell stare to the mirthless smile to the pained grimace.

I'm not going to lie. *Driven to Kill* isn't THAT bad of a Seagal movie. I'd put it squarely in the middle of his direct-to-video fodder. If that were to translate into some sort of stars rating it would be 2 stars. One for the movie and one for the viewer who had enough moxy to make it through this sad tripe.

Dmitry Chepovetsky who plays Lanie's fiance and Seagal's sidekick is an utter trainwreck. I've seen better emoting from a Claymation film than what this man is able to provide, and he STILL outclasses Seagal in every single scene they have together. You know the film is bad when you long for anyone to speak whose name isn't Steven Seagal.

The acting-what there was of it-isn't this film's only atrocity. The plot of the movie was tissue thin and so full of WTF that I stopped repeating WTF out loud after about 20 minutes. I got tired of hearing myself say it. For instance, the big finale showdown takes place at a hospital. All of the bad guys are converging on Seagal and someone he's trying to protect at a hospital. To clear the place out a little bit someone pulls a fire alarm. What happens? Doctors, nurses, aids and technicians run like mad. Does anyone try to evacuate the patients? Nope. Not even one of those poor bastards are moved. I guess the line of thinking is every man for himself at the hospital. Does the fire department show up? Nope.

Next there were the gun fights. Well, that's not exactly correct. There's gunfire, and lots of it. But is it exciting? No, no it isn't because people just walk into frame and start spraying bullets for very long periods of time. Rarely is anyone actually shooting at a discernible target. It's just one guy Rambo style bullet spraying with a pause so that the other guy can jump out and ratttattat his bullets. Stuff gets shot up. Things shatter and bullets whiz ping around but absolutely nothing about it builds tension, concern or excitement. During one of the many boring gunfire battles I found myself contemplating when the last time I was that I had a descent bowel movement.

Cops in these sorts of movies are pretty dumb. They're constantly two or three steps behind what's going on because, naturally, if they had brains and actual police skills the bad guys and the good guys would both be arrested and the story would be over, but dear baby Jesus in a blanket, these cops were flipping IDIOTS. They go from one body littered crime scene to the next scratching their heads like they can't figure it out, even when they've caught both parties red handed! Oh, but wait! There's more! Ruslan actually calls the cops himself to spell things out for them and tell them to go here or go there or the bad guys are over in this other place doing this other thing. It's just complete ridiculousness.

Seagal actually runs a little bit in this movie and has some fights. The fight choreography is cropped really close though so you can see his hands waving around and such, but you never get a good, clear impression of the fight. Throw in a healthy batch of super quick cut editing and there's no real flow to the fight, no drama because you can't even tell who's doing what. Still, the fighting in *Driven to Kill* is leaps and bounds above what Seagal does in later films so I guess we can all be somewhat thankful for at least having that.

Something I noticed is that a lot of Seagal movies have seedy bar/stripper joint/lap dance scenes just randomly inserted in them. In this one they go to said establishment and when Seagal's sidekick inquires as to why they're there, Seagal answers that they are hunting bad guys and bad guys are hunting them so if they just sit still a while the bad guys will just, you know, find them and save a lot of hassle. So, I'm wondering "Ok, so the bad guys just think...where could they be? Ohhh, of course, they're over at the strip joint just waiting for us to show up and shoot up the place and have a knife fight or two." Well, that's exactly what happens. Doesn't make a lick worth of sense but there you go. Also, Seagal and his buddy are sitting there with a naked lady humping around a pole and they're chatting away about the people they've shot up, seemingly without a concern that the pole lady might go fetch the police or tell someone. OK, right.

I wanted to laugh my ass off at *Driven to Kill* but I didn't. I made the mistake of watching a more recent movie of his called A GOOD MAN before seeing this one. After witnessing Seagal in that, this one took on the appearance of Citizen Kane by comparison. For anyone else, *Driven to Kill* may be what you feel like doing when you discover what you've wasted your money and life on. Proceed with caution!

–Charles E. Pratt, Jr.

The Keeper (2009)

The Keeper was directed by Keoni Waxman and stars Steven Seagal as Roland Sallinger. *The Keeper*, an Action/Crime/Thriller movie, was Waxman's first feature film collaboration with Steven Seagal. After *The Keeper*, Waxman's and Seagal's collaboration would continue for eight motion pictures and eight television episodes of *True Justice*. *The Keeper* first premiered in October of 2009 in Japan and was released straight to DVD in the USA a few months later.

Roland (Seagal) is a cop who is shot by his corrupt partner (Brian Keith Gamble) in an assassination attempt during a drug bust and miraculously survives. In a series of fortuitous events, Roland survives again when his partner comes to finish the job at the hospital. As Roland heals from his wounds, he finds that he has been medically retired from the police force. It is then that an old friend Conner Wells (Steph DuVall) contacts Roland for help after a foiled kidnapping attempt on Conner's daughter Nikita (Liezl Carstens) and asks Roland to be her bodyguard, which he agrees. Nikita eventually is successfully kidnapped by henchmen working for Jason Cross (Luce Rains) over Uranium mining rights. Roland eventually finds Nikita and saves the day.

Part of what makes a movie great is being emotionally invested in what happens to the characters during their journey. The Keeper offers little to the moviegoer in this category. Following Roland's character arc, we find that there are problems. At the beginning of the film, Roland is a cop who is mortally wounded. Roland being mortally wounded at the beginning of the film had no bearing to the rest of his story. An interesting twist would have been if his injuries somehow made Roland more vulnerable as he faced adversity, but it never happens. We are also told that Roland and Conner are 'old friends' but are provided no back story so later in the story when it is revealed that Conner and the antagonist Jason Cross are 'old friends', too, it's more than a bit fishy how Roland never knew of Jason Cross as he and Conner were (supposedly) so close. No background is given on Roland other than he is a cop who was medically retired. There was no background on how Roland became a skilled fighter. Roland's abilities are just assumed, and the viewer is asked to blindly accept that. Nikita's character arc is similarly troubling. Arguably, in the order of importance, her story importance should be second only to Roland's. Nikita is the kidnap victim and, ideally, the moviegoer should fear for her safety and it's difficult to feel anything but indifference for her. Nikita's boyfriend Mason Silver (Arron Shiver) is a womanizing drug addict, anything but a picture of trust. Nikita stands by as eyewitness to these occurrences by Mason multiple times throughout the movie and Nikita still runs back to him time and again. As a moviegoer, it's hard to feel for her safety when she climbs into Mason's vehicle in blind trust and then who is eventually hand delivered to the kidnappers. And then there's the antagonist, Jason Cross. In the second and third act of the film, Cross's henchmen engage is some light bullying and were involved in a kidnapping plot - not very dastardly. The worst Jason does himself is extort money from his ex-business partner, Conner Wells. Jason Cross does nothing in The Keeper to make us hate the character or wish injury upon him. This is important as there will be no satisfactory payoff for the viewer when the antagonist is finally defeated. Definitely not the typical Steven Seagal movie antagonist character arc of days past.

Keoni Waxman took liberties with the story that were very convenient. At the beginning of the movie, just after Roland was shot by his partner, he lay in a hospital bed unconscious...or so we are told by the nursing staff. Roland's niece Regina Lawson (Trine Christensen) comes to visit and lays her purse on the bedside table which had a gun inside of it - very convenient. Roland, seemingly tricking hospital staff by being conscious the whole time, takes advantage of this convenience and takes the gun from the purse which he later uses to defend himself in a second assassination attempt by his partner.

Mason is a up and coming boxer and his character is built as a macho, confident man early in the film.

Jason Cross's henchmen have way too easy of a time extracting information from Manson, a man who registers his fists as lethal weapons. Mason's weakness in that moment eventually leads to Nikita's successful kidnapping. And then there's the kidnapping scene itself. When Roland was charged as Nikita's bodyguard, he gave her a tracking necklace so he would always know where she was. During the kidnap scene, an unconvincing struggle takes place between Nikita and a henchman with the necklace conveniently ripped off her neck and flung out the window of the fleeing getaway vehicle.

The lure of Steven Seagal's films is the way he dispatches of the less-than-capable henchmen via hand-to-hand combat (or by firearm) which ultimately leads to the subsequent dispatching of a semi-capable lead henchman or boss. In Steven Seagal's early work, his best work, the character arcs of the antagonist typically led to satisfyingly bone breaking scenes of mayhem as Steven works his way through the help to eventually remove the antagonist in fantastic, gruesome fashion. *The Keeper* offers no such satisfaction to the moviegoer. Sure, there are glimpses of hand-to-hand combat and gun battles to further the plot but in *The Keeper*, Steven only fights characters with no serious character arcs and the antagonist lives to fight another day. This is opposite of what was reminiscent in his best work.

Now this is not to say that Steven didn't turn in a believable performance. In *The Keeper*, Steven is in his comfort zone: A cop who is skilled in hand-to-hand combat who doesn't seem to miss when shooting at the bad guys. It is without question that Steven Seagal is a master of martial arts - his body of work is testament to this fact. This said, age may be a contributing factor in how much action is in this film. In Steven's early work, he was imposing and brutal - enemies were absolutely crushed which is a testament to his youth. In The Keeper, Steven has more shooting scenes than actual hand to hand combat scenes and while he wins those physical fights, he seemed much less imposing and brutal. In his personal life, Steven is a collector of custom pistols, is an avid shooter and with well documented pistol accuracy. Steven has also worked with law enforcement agencies in Louisiana, New Mexico and Texas working in varying roles.

–Pat Kawula

A Dangerous Man (2009)

A Dangerous Man is a direct-to-video movie written and directed by Keoni Waxman and stars Steven Seagal as Shane, a wrongfully convicted man recently released from prison. Shane attempts to start a new life in Bellingham, Washington, but things go haywire when he witnesses the murder of a police officer by Chinese mobsters. Shane meets a woman named Tia (Marlaina Mah) who is being hunted by the mobsters because her uncle is trying to escape China and live peacefully in the United States. Shane agrees to help her and soon forges an alliance with Russian mobsters to battle the Chinese mobsters.

The movie opens with Shane protecting his wife from a potential carjacking. We see Shane chase the carjacker and then we flash forward to learn that the carjacker is dead. This is where we discover that Shane used to be with Special Forces and possesses the skills to kill people like the carjacker. Shane doesn't lawyer up, goes to prison, and is dumped by his wife days before he is to be released due to the tireless work of the Innocence Project. Shane is disillusioned and doesn't know how he can go on living in an unjust world.

Waxman has the right ingredients for a perfect movie with the plight of Shane, a wrongfully convicted man. Shane could attempt to reconnect with his wife and find out who killed the carjacker. Maybe he uncovers something sinister in the town like a corrupt police organization. Maybe during Shane's Special Forces days he killed someone's dad or brother and the carjacking was just a set-up to get revenge on Shane. There could be a moment where Shane must work with someone in law enforcement and there is that seething resentment, but that doesn't happen. Instead, *A Dangerous Man* goes off in a different direction where the prison backstory has no use.

Shane's wrongful conviction is pointless, and his wife is shown after the carjacking but only in topless flashbacks. Also, nothing is ever explained about the death of the carjacker. The cops that had it out for Shane during the questioning are never seen again.

The same day Shane is released from prison, he gets into a fight outside a liquor store with two punks running their mouths. They are beaten within an inch of their lives. Shane knows he messed up because he goes back in the store and steals the tape with the security footage. Shane then steals a car the two loudmouths were trying to sell outside the store and heads to a rest stop where he decides to think about life while downing a bottle of whiskey.

We then cut to a freighter in the Pacific and there are Chinese immigrants on board. There is an elderly Chinese man on the ship, and it seems that he is important to the story, but the opportunity is pretty much wasted with little or no clear explanation. He is apprehended on the shore by some angry Chinese men who push him into a car.

Sergey (Jesse Hutch) and his drunk buddy, show up at the rest stop following a big night of drinking and Shane observes them from a distance. Then a police officer pulls over a car with two Chinese men at the same rest stop. The officer dies when he pops the trunk of the car to find cash and the body of a young woman. Sergey and his buddy witness the murder and are hunted down by the killers. The buddy is killed, but Shane helps Sergey escape, and they grab the woman and the money.

To Shane and Sergey's surprise, the woman is alive. Her name is Tia and she confesses that her uncle was being smuggled in to the United States from China. The Chinese mafia wants the uncle for some reason because he's the accountant who knows everything about the giant drug operation in the 'Golden Triangle'. Tia admits that a Chinese mobster arranged for her uncle to come to America. Shane and Tia are dropped off in town and Sergey tells Shane to look for him if they need help.

We soon discover that the cops are connected to the Chinese mafia. The Chinese mafia boss, Chen (Terry Chen), runs the show and is working with a real piece of work known as The Colonel (Byron Mann). Chen isn't believable as a mafia boss. He's not someone who strikes fear into the hearts of viewers. He comes off as some douche who shows up at the drunk at the Olive Garden with a party of ten people at closing time and spends the majority of the night sexually harassing the hostess.

Shane and Tia discover they are being followed by the Chinese mafia and they're going to need help. Shane doesn't have time for the cops, so he looks for Sergey. Vlad (Vitaliy Kravchenko) is Sergey's father and is the top Russian mobster in town. Sergey tells Vlad how Shane saved his life, so Vlad is indebted to Shane for this courageous act. Both men form an alliance to take down the Chinese mafia and the crooked cops. The remainder of a movie is a shootout at Vlad's house that leads to the ultimate showdown at Chen's warehouse. The uncle and Tia are reunited and Seagal moves to Russia.

While at times, it is somewhat entertaining, *A Dangerous Man* fails to deliver a solid movie. Shane's backstory has nothing to do with the plot, and it would have made more sense if the crooked cops or the Chinese mafia sent Shane to jail for killing the carjacker. Also, Seagal wins every fight in this movie easily. The protagonist needs to face major obstacles and viewers love a bit of suspense, which is lacking. Watching this movie is the equivalent of playing a video game on easy mode. Finally, this movie was definitely hard to watch.

–Tony Doug Wright

Steven Seagal: Law Man (2009 – 2010, 2014)

The very first thing you notice when you begin watching Steven Seagal's bizarre but entertaining venture into reality television – well, besides the fact that the dude who once said, "I'm gonna take you to the bank…to the blood bank" is a cop – is that so much of the show is full of shaky cam. Even during office sequences where no action or tension building is required.

As episodes of the immortal *Steven Seagal: Lawman* unfold before your disbelieving eyes, you start to get a picture of what Officer - er, DEPUTY CHIEF Seagal is really about; most entertainingly, quotes by himself ABOUT himself, such as how Zen he is and how that comes in super handy when he is out nabbin' suspects who thought they could operate above the law.

One sequence finds him slapping handcuffs onto a very upset dude while saying, without irony, "This gentleman is not a very good Zen practitioner." He speaks intermittently and at great length about his own usage of using Zen to shoot guns; he specifically refers to this as "Asian Zen lesson in gun shooting" and quotes Sun Tzu liberally and with a raised, knowing eyebrow.

This comes into play a couple episodes in when he gets all Zen-like by pointing a gun at a suspect's head while the guy is calmly walking up into his own driveway with a couple bags of groceries. Moments like that help us to truly understand why Alan Sepinwall of the Star Ledger once referred to Deputy Chief Seagal as an "accidental comedy savant. He earns that badge more and more as the series plays out, sometimes by, let's say, appropriating Ebonics in certain company, sounding not at all at home or natural while squinting out lines like, "You ain't have to worry about him, brotha. He gone."

Which is not to say that there aren't moments where you can't help but admire him. His sticktuitiveness, his dedication, his insistence on keeping his hair the exact same way for *so many years* (sort of like Dracula if Dracula had a little ponytail and competed with Bruce Willis for the title of squinting and looking off in thought or disgust).

He also does still possess some of that charisma that made him an action hero way back in the day. In fact, I watched several episodes with my daughter Audri, and once she walked in while he was playing blues guitar on stage and said, stunned, "What the hell? He plays guitar? Wait…he's actually kinda good, I don't know if I hate him or think he's ethereal!"

That's right, we get some footage of Deputy Chief Seagal jammin' out some decent guitar for the righteous endeavor of raising money for a children's hospital. He plays guitar like he does so many things (including, according to former co-star John Leguizamo, running): in an unorthodox way. He uses his right thumb as a pick, and even while sitting down, he holds the guitar with the rest of his massive hand as if the strap won't hold it up without his mighty help.

His interactions with civilians are sometimes befuddling, sometimes astonishing, always fascinating. He rolls into a crime scene and seems to expect the inevitable requests for autographs and even takes the rare jibe with a weird sort of conceited humility:

"My auntie loves your movies."

"You don't?"

"I don't watch 'em."

He dismisses that perceived slight from a complete stranger with a bit of a half-smile and that ever present Zen-filled knowing look, intimating that she probably *would* love them if she ever took the time to watch them.

And yes, he is even occasionally funny on purpose, such as when he gets recognized and asks the person if he can borrow $5.

Still, more prevalent are stumbling comedy situations where, after a guy with a Jason Voorhees mask is tased and stuck into the back of a police car by Steven Seagal, Deputy Chief Seagal holds the Jason mask up to his fellow officers and informs them that it is a "marking of someone who's fixin' to do bad things."

In total, there are nearly 30 episodes of *Steven Seagal: Lawman*, which aired over 5 years in 3 seasons for two different networks. Five of those have never aired, mercifully, some might say. My answer to that is that this show is somewhat addicting, despite yourself, despite the absolute knowledge that what you are watching is part action hero historical document and part television train wreck.

Those episodes presumably didn't air because of an infamous occurrence in which a police team, accompanied by Seagal, drove a tank into the home of a man who was suspected of animal cruelty via cock-fighting which ironically allegedly resulted in killing hundreds of roosters and a puppy.

Yes, that really did happen.

Deputy Chief Seagal, alas, resigned rather than face an Internal Affairs investigation by the Jefferson Parish Sheriff's office into the not very Zen allegations of sex trafficking and sexual assault raised in a 2010 lawsuit by an ex-employee. It should be noted that the lawsuit was dropped. The details behind that dismissal are foggy; did she settle with Zen Drac?

So many more entertaining details and soul-crushingly adept Seagal triumphs await you in *Steven Seagal: Lawman*. Is it true that he is a blade master? Yes, pretty much, as it turns out. Can he shoot a gun? The tip off a matchstick(!), and also laments that he failed because he was trying to light the match with the bullet, much to the agape-mouthed bemusement of the officer being blessed by his Asian Zen gun lesson. He also appears to be a sort of romance advisor and a bit of a dog whisperer, too.

Should you spend a Saturday night binge watching Deputy Chief Steven Seagal as he regales you with his philosophies, pals up with a rescue Pitbull for an impromptu 20-minute sequel to *Turner and Hooch*, takes an officer to a Chinese acupuncturist, surprises his wife (and us, sorta) with romantic aplomb on Valentine's Day, and tries to heal sick officers against their will with his ancient remedies (yes, that ALL happens)?

I mean, why not? After all, Seagal has a no-knock warrant, a bottle of rum culled from the evidence locker, and the password to your favorite streaming service. Probably.

–Paul Counelis

Machete (2010)

Machete is amazing. As an action fan, this movie has it all. Originally, Robert Rodriguez claimed that he came up with the idea of the character after seeing Danny Trejo on the set of *Desperado*. The idea then turned into a trailer played between the Rodriguez and Tarantino *Grindhouse* films. In 2010, that idea finally came into fruition when *Machete* was made into a full-blown feature length film. Not only that, but the movie was also filled with a star-studded cast including Robert De Niro, Jeff Fahey, Don Johnson, Michelle Rodriguez, Jessica Alba, Lindsay Lohan, and Cheech Marin. It also made a total of $44 million worldwide. This movie had it all. Fighting? Check. Explosions? Check. Crazy amount of a violence? Checks all around. Machete is everything and more as an action film. But I'm not here to give a general review of the movie as a whole. While I highly recommend watching it, this is all about Steven Seagal playing the role of Rogelio Torrez, the Federale-turned-drug lord villain.

The biggest surprise for me regarding this film is that Steven Seagal agreed to play the bad guy. While he has taken on anti-hero type roles before, this was something completely different than what he usually portrays on the screen. There doesn't seem to be a difference in his acting from any of his other projects, but he seems to fit the role perfectly. I'm sure Seagal would have people believing it was all because of his acting skills but something tells me Rodriguez knew exactly what to do when casting him. We are introduced to how evil Torrez is in the first few minutes of the film. It opens with Machete trying to save a woman only to find out that it was a ploy to take him out. Torrez shows up with Machete's wife and immediately decapitates her in front of him. Talk about an opening for a film.

While Seagal doesn't have as much screen time as De Niro or Fahey, he brings just as much hatred to his character as the others do throughout the film. Anyone watching it wants to see these vile and devious characters receive their punishment. But none is more deserving than to finally see Trejo dish it out to Seagal at the end of the film.

Seagal plays the role well. It fits him perfectly – he's an over-the-top character in an over-the-top film. Torrez is truly unlikable and does not leave any room for sympathy from the viewer. As he checks in with Fahey's character throughout the film, the audience knowingly waits for him to make his presence known to Machete. When the two finally meet again wielding their weapons of choice, the audience is expecting fireworks. While we don't get a huge grand finale, it is still pleasing nonetheless to see Machete come out on top.

The fight scene between the two is like many other Seagal films later in his career – close-ups, body doubles, and camera cuts with jerky motions. But the best part comes when Machete sticks his blade through Torrez's stomach. Rather than letting Machete finish him off, Torrez gets a few words in and then performs seppuku. Another win for the good guys. But there was something about that final fight that stayed with me – was this how it was originally written? Or did Seagal have a final say in his death? It seems like a Seagal thing to do. Why? Because even while dying with a machete sticking through him, Torrez states that he could still kill Machete but would rather not do it. Then again, maybe Robert Rodriguez is so good at what he does that he's convinced us otherwise.

Seagal looks like his typical self throughout the film. It would not be surprising if we found out that Seagal provided all of his own wardrobe. Or, if he did have to get fitted for costumes, it was probably written into his contract that he got to keep everything. Regardless of the costumes, Seagal comes in sporting his patented hairstyle and sunglasses. But we cannot forget about his acting. It is not uncommon for Seagal to have some sort of accent. Here, he has a Spanish accent. And oh, what an accent. Seagal allegedly fired his accent coach because he was afraid the lesson was going too well, and that people would not recognize him on screen. I sincerely hope this is true because it just adds to the mystique of Steven Seagal.

One of the more positive sides coming from his portrayal of Torrez came when many reviews pointed out that this was the first time Seagal had been in a full theatrical release since his time in 2002's *Half Past Dead*. Some even wondered if this would be a turnaround for his career. While we already know the answer to that question, Seagal himself didn't seem to let any of that faze him. During an interview for the film, Seagal stated he was very happy with being involved in the project and seemed to be in on the wackiness of the movie. He knew it was crazy and he still wanted to be a part of it. While it is normal for actors to take roles seriously, it was actually surprising to see Seagal speak on it without being his usual self. He spoke about how great of a time he had with it and even pointed out the important immigration message in the film.

–John Bruske

Born to Raise Hell (2010)

There's really only one problem with 2010's *Born to Raise Hell* starring Steven Seagal. Unfortunately, it happens to be Steven Seagal, which also happens to be the only reason the movie exists. A direct-to-DVD mobius strip indeed.

Truthfully, I've seen worse movies. Shit, I've seen worse Seagal movies. So I was thoroughly prepared for the shit storm that is a Seagal production. All of the elements were there; two-dimensional characters playing out a one-dimensional plot riddled with multiple "are you fucking kidding me?" holes. Seagal plays Bobby Samuels, the head of an IDTF team in Bucharest. IDTF stands for International Drug Task Force, an English acronym that makes no sense in Eastern Europe, but details like that are a distraction you cannot get bogged down with when set to endure the Seagal experience. Naturally, we learn early on that Bobby's partner was killed and "headquarters" has sent a replacement named Steve, played by D. Neil Mark, who might as well have been wearing a red *Star Trek* security uniform. Just to be sure, I kept referring to him as DOA Steve. Just to underscore that Steve isn't making it to the end credits, he informs us at an oddly inopportune time that his wife is eight months pregnant, and he'd really like to make it home to see his kid get born. Oh, DOA Steve. So naive.

Nonetheless, as we watch Bobby lumber through the nightclubs and back alleys of Bucharest in search of drug kingpin Costel, played by Darren Shahlavi, I began to wonder if the cameras had just tagged along with Seagal as he went clubbing. "Damn it! Seagal is going to the bathroom again so just keep shooting. We'll make it work later!" The dialogue, which I'm being kind in referring to it that way, also seems to be retrofitted. Pretty much everyone else has their lines, knows their character and works toward the plot. It occurred to me that instead of D-level actors in an F-level movie, this cast may have been truly the greatest improv troop known to modern cinema. Everyone else had their characters, knew their lines and attempted to advance the story; everyone that is except Seagal, whose dialogue seemed to be truly improvised. You could see the "what the fuck did he just say?" look in their eyes as they attempted to respond to the mush-mouth lines delivered at them in Seagal's deliberately obtuse style.

But hey, it's a Seagal movie, right? No one comes in expecting Oscar-worthy performances. Although, I do think the editor might be worthy of an award. The "action" sequences consist of tight close-ups of Seagal's face and upper torso, followed by distant shots of the obvious stunt double doing the actual work. I can only imagine the hours of work in the editing room trying to piece that jigsaw puzzle together in any coherent manner. But any thought of acknowledging that feat is washed away by the plethora of completely useless sequences that are spliced in for no apparent reason. A close-up of a cop walking out of the station. Must be an important plot point right? Especially considering that his action is seen in slow-motion. What is going to happen? Will he be ambushed? Is he a bad guy? We'll never know because the entire shot served absolutely no fucking purpose whatsoever! Just a cop leaving the station. What's next? A detective taking a crap? (which would be an apt metaphor for this film) A secretary getting a Snickers bar? Actually, that might be more interesting.

The cinematographer also made some interesting choices, using a deliberate blur and stop-action method to give a hallucinatory effect to many shots. Many, many shots. So many shots in fact, that I'm not sure the cinematographer wasn't just tripping on mushrooms in order to make it through the shoot. But could you really blame him? I know I wished I had some shrooms to make it easier.

But back to the "action." In addition to being a drug kingpin, Costel is also a sadistic prick who likes to rape and murder female victims after he and his gang burst into their homes. Even though he obviously derives his income, including that to run his nightclub, from dealing dope, he apparently likes to rape and murder as a side gig. You know, for fun. As Bobby begins to chase down Costel, we get a glimpse of our hero's home life. Naturally, he's living with a beautiful 20-something who just can't keep her hands off of Seagal. As she disrobes and reveals her lithe and toned body, Seagal almost breaks the fourth wall and looks into the camera as if to say, "It's good to be me!" (I know you'll be just as shocked as I was that he wrote the script) However, I couldn't help but get the same vibe as when Jabba the Hutt disgustingly licks his lips while ready to enjoy Princess Leia. Of course, that analogy isn't rather exact as Jabba was in slightly better shape.

As the story builds towards a merciful conclusion, the death of DOA Steve finally makes its preordained appearance. Despite Bobby telling Steve to hang back during an earlier raid because he was an impending dad, when the final showdown comes, he practically uses Steve as a human shield and places him on point heading into the bad guy's den. So when DOA takes a bullet to the neck, it seems to be curtains for him until Seagal moves in and tells his partner to stop his own bleeding ("press hard" Really? Gee, thanks buddy. But then he leaves him for no actual reason other than to let him die alone, which is how I felt as I watched this disaster of a movie. And again, the only disaster in this movie is Seagal, which I suppose is the point.

For all the criticism, Seagal did make the movie possible, providing jobs and spreading out the surprisingly large $10 million budget. Although one can't help but wonder what percentage of that went to craft services.

–Jon Arking

"Sheep Impact" (2010)

I have never met Steven Seagal...but I almost did.

When Carlton United Breweries announced a competition to submit a wild 'over a beer' story, in which your part in said tale would be portrayed by Steven Seagal, my heart fluttered spasmodically.

Above the Law, Out for Justice, Hard to Kill...damn I loved that movie. Seagal was the one trick ponytail that kept on delivering like an Adam Sandler movie. You know, how they're all about the same guy, an outsider and an underdog that eventually makes good. Well Seagal was the tough cat with the slick hair; he talked in one-liners (as did most of his contemporaries) and through guys, who thought they had bigger balls, from pillar to post until they spilled their guts and gave up Richie Madano.

By 2010 the ponytail was long gone, along with most of his credibility. Seagal had transformed into a pudgy caricature of Mason Storm, rather than a majestic Gran-Daddy of action. To this end he sought solace in the Stright-to-DVD Underverse, and from his nose-bleed seats, he'd show the world that he still had what it took...that he was indeed alive, and aikido-kicking.

I remember submitting at least 10 stories to the comp. Didn't win of course, but some chap called Paul Wieland did. Thus resulting in that which has come to be remembered as "Sheep Impact", directed by Brendon Gibbons (*Pre-Occupied*, 2014) and filmed in Arizona, doubling for Down Under. (Like we're hard up for desolate wilderness in Australia...? Still these Hollywood folks will have their way.)

"You're bein' a tool mate," is a line that strikes me, coming from the spray-tanned, sloppy-looking grand master as both he and another bloke, Craig (Martin Copping, *Zombie Hunter*), seem hell-bent on impressing a girl, Sarah Beachwood (Kirsty Lee Allan, *CSI: NY*). Craig's plan was to bring meat to her barbie. But being unable to deliver the goods, Craig and Seagal proceed to engage in a triumphant moment of toxic-moronity, when out of the Never Never a sheep appears as seemingly the answer to the prayers of Segal's tool-of-a-mate.

Violence is not the answer, and Segal rescues the sheep from the edge of darkness, only to then be reprimanded by a local copper (Jonathon Buckley, *ZOOMBIES 2*) for pre-supposed nefarious intent. Old man Steve uses his connection to the plain of enlightenment to communicate with the puzzled sheep, weaponizing it, and using the moment the sheep takes down the law man as an excuse to run, awkwardly, back to the car and get the *flock* outta there.

So then to the barbie, and there are no gourmet cuts to impress. The sexy hostess isn't fazed; turns out the local law enforcement officer from earlier is also one of the party dwellers, and he's carrying a big knife, readying himself to meet the meat situation head on. Suddenly, the sheep calls to Seagal from the astral plain. Segal walks around the back of the shed and into action, uncovering the dastardly plot of the local copper to murder the same sheep he seemed committed to protecting.

What ensues is a bit of half-assed aikido and an ending we might have bought happening to old man Steve twenty years ago, but really, him just being in this thing is enough to make Carlton a fortune...isn't it? So the resolution sees Seagal getting the girl and his tool mate ending up with this chick, Rachel (Jessica Godber, *Alice in Wonderland*, 2010/1) who has her glass eye on him. The sheep lives, so it's Palm Sunday all round.

So what you ask, does this have to do with me not quite meeting Steven Seagal?

See, around the same time I was a struggling screenwriter who found himself in the Big Smoke (Brisbane) for a meeting that would see my services procured to write another movie that would probably never get made (but that's another story). I was to enjoy a breakfast (at the behest of my new potential employer) at the Marriot, and as I made my way through the lobby (having ascended from the underground carpark), it was impossible not to notice a cacophony of crowded people and cameras slowly making their way from the front door to the footpath.

I was instructed to sit anywhere I pleased, so I did, and it was between washing down a mouthful of Eggs Benedict with apple juice and picking up my coffee, that I asked a passing waitress as to the nature of the disturbance in the foyer?

"Steven Segal just checked out," she said.

"No shit?" was my reply.

"Matter of fact, he just ate breakfast in the same seat you're sitting in…"

The warmth of the chair beneath me, took on new meaning and for a moment I heard William Smith's voice in my head, "Once, giants lived in the Earth, Conan." But this giant had fallen hard; he was the new face of Carlton Dry. While the fresh blood in Hollywood had their foundations and their fragrances, here *we* were, Steven Seagal and I, two warriors fighting a losing battle against the movie business…me with my Eggs Benedict and old man Steve with his beer.

–Kent Hill

Maximum Conviction (2010)

I don't think I've heard the phrase, "My favorite Steven Seagal movie" in decades. It's tough to think about when someone turns themselves into a cosmic joke. Look, he had legitimate hits at the beginning of his career, but even those haven't aged very well. When it comes to his later movies, which have been direct-to-video for longer than I can remember, you rarely even hear things like "guilty pleasure" or "so bad it's good." It all just falls into the "He's still doing this?" category. This is why I'm here to blow your minds. *Maximum Conviction* is my favorite Steven Seagal movie.

I know, I get it. You're confused, upset, and even possibly enraged. Here's the thing, though. It's my favorite, because it showcases the overblown oaf for the absurdity that he truly is. Oddly enough, it's surrounded by enough actual entertainment that it makes the movie present like a double edged sword. One side is sharp enough to cut through a tomato like a Ginsu, and the other looks like it was used to hammer cinder blocks.

Let's get to the story. A secret military prison is being decommissioned in Oregon. A handful of male prisoners are locked up in the remaining functional cell block, and another block has been temporarily reopened to house two female prisoners. Manning ("Stone Cold" Steve Austin) is already on the scene overseeing what the real Steve Austin might call a clustermuck. He seems to have it all under control when his partner, or boss, or supervisor, Cross (Seagal) shows up to discuss the mission. Honestly, I couldn't figure out the true relationship between these two. Have you ever tried to make slime with your kid, but you put the glue in a bowl, then add contact lens solution, and no matter how much you stir it up, it just doesn't want to turn into slime? That's the on-screen chemistry between Seagal and Austin. It never comes together.

Anyway, Cross lays out the plan for the next morning, they talk to the warden, and Cross decides to take his team to a nearby bar. Manning says he'll meet them there at six, because he has to make sure everything is locked down for the night. There's one problem. A garbage truck is stuck to a compactor, or some such nonsense, and the driver can't leave until he gets it detached. Manning has to get under the machine and fix it. There's only one problem. Are you ready? Nothing is wrong with it! This isn't a garbage truck. It's a Trojan horse for a mercenary team.

I know! I'm as excited as you are. They explode their way out, Manning takes out a couple of them, and he runs off into the prison. Here's the kicker. Right before that, a guy named Blake (Michael Paré) shows up pretending to be transport for the two incarcerated women. The truth is that one of the women carries top secret information, and Blake needs to take her out. Guards get killed, Blake cuts off the warden's finger, and he ends up watching most of the action from a security booth. Ultimately, as you'd expect, the story culminates in the ultimate showdown between Blake and Cross. A fight for the ages! Or, maybe the aged.

Most of the supporting characters are your typical action movie clichés, but once things get going, it's generally nonstop battle. While you don't expect a classically trained thespian out of Steve Austin, he does a solid job in his fight scenes, and they don't lean too heavily on his wrestling moves, which is nice. Michael Paré is my favorite part of the movie. He seems like he's having a great time being the villain. He even sells his fight with Seagal, and making that fool look good is not easy.

So, let's get to the Kung Fu Hustler, Chunk Norris, The Karate Kaiju. The true Steven Seagal shines through in this entire movie. I'll go step by step.

He's a terrible actor. In his first scene with Austin, Seagal attempts some sort of horrific Cajun accent. That goes away for the bulk of the story, where he mumbles his way through so badly that I almost turned on the captions. I ultimately decided that it was worth not knowing what was going on so that I could experience the full Seagal. At the end, during the last conversation with Austin, he does another accent, sort of. I can't even describe it, because it resembles no human sound.

He can't fight. Seagal has two big fight scenes. In the first, he battles a huge inmate who would ordinarily destroy him. He somehow takes the guy down with a weak clap to both of his ears. This useless move is used multiple times for some reason. In his final fight with Blake, he throws ankle high kicks and slow punches that make him look like a winded granny. Just like in his live demonstrations, he has to pay people to lose fights to him.

He thinks he's a ladies' man. Samantha (Steph Song) is the prisoner with the classified secrets. She's a CIA informant who handles herself well in this crazy situation. In the end, though, she turns into some giggling sorority girl who skips off with Cross with clear overtones that she's ready to mount his bloated grunting carcass. The fact that Song didn't vomit her way through that scene is miraculous.

He pretends to be a lawman, but he's really a scumbag. Cross works as a government contractor for the police and the military, but in the end, he takes a huge bundle of cash that Blake stole, and he splits it with Manning. In reality show mode, Seagal is an actual cop, but whether you look at the time he drove a tank through an elderly couple's home with convicted felon and former sheriff Joe Arpaio, the many allegations of sexual harassment, or his general bad behavior, we're not dealing with a model citizen.

So, there it is. The most Steven Seagal movie ever made. It really is my favorite of his, and I say that, of course, with *Maximum Conviction*.

I had to. I'm not sorry about it, either.

–Kevin Moyers

True Justice (2010 – 2012)

How do you even begin writing a review like this? I have spent roughly 1,170 minutes watching Steven Seagal. I don't believe too many others can say the same thing. Where do I even begin?

True Justice is only two seasons. Like any ill-fated television series, it was left on a cliffhanger without finding out what happens at the end. The series starts off with Elijah Kane (Seagal) and his group of undercover police officers. Then, it becomes a series based on Elijah Kane and his undercover rogue agents working with the CIA. Yes, it went from police officers to Non-CIA, CIA agents within two seasons. Don't worry if that doesn't make any sense. Trust me when I say that the writing is completely different between the two seasons. Steven Seagal and Joe Halpin wrote the first season while Keoni Waxman and Richard Beattie wrote a majority of the second one. When a series changes writers, small nuances from season to season can pop up but not enough to detract from the show. True Justice is not that case. The seasons were absurdly different from one another. The one common ground throughout *True Justice* is that many of the episodes were made to be watched in two parts.

The first episode was reportedly written solely by Seagal. There is no question that this is his writing. Why? Because it sounds exactly like something an older man would write when thinking about how younger characters would act. It seems as if Seagal simply refused to fact check any of his writing, shooting down the editor for any factual inconsistencies while claiming that he knows what it's like on the streets. It's like watching a whole hour of a "Fellow Kids" meme.

That being said, I still enjoyed watching the first season, even with all of its mild annoyances and questionable writing. How can a series starring Steven be annoying? Well, throughout the first season, Steven does a unique New Orleans/Seattle accent, while trying to make sure he did not enunciate half of his words. Further, one woman's terrible New York accent magically disappears after the first episode. Don't even get me started on the Russian accents throughout the whole series. It's a sight to behold. Like something that came out of a bad 1950s noir film. But what about the first season as a whole story?

In the first season, Steven has a team underneath him in an undercover unit at the Seattle Police Department. Forget about any legality concerns in this television series. Throw it all out the door. It isn't too far off from other cop show dramas. There's repeated talk about Camp Harmony, an old internment camp outside of Seattle. One would be led to believe this is an allegory but don't give the writing that much credit. Throughout the season, Seagal's background as Elijah Kane is slowly brought out. He had a family – a Japanese wife and children. I mention this because Kane tells us his wife's family was in the internment camp that keeps getting referenced throughout the episodes. However, the family background is murky – the viewer is to believe that Kane's wife passed away from an illness. Or she divorced Kane because of spending all of his time on his job. Or that she passed away, again, from something completely different. It's never truly known what happened because it's never mentioned again in Season Two.

Kane has a decent team underneath him, as well as a new rookie that doesn't understand how to work in the Special Investigation Unit. It's no surprise to see this rookie cop learn and mature throughout the season under the tutelage of Kane. The main plot of Season One is the team trying to figure out how drugs are coming into Seattle while maintaining the peace. They run into various gang members, a serial killer, a copycat killer, adult entertainers, corrupted cops, corrupted attorneys, corrupted military, corrupted government agencies and agents, terrorists, hostile American citizens, pedophiles, rapists, creeps, Russian mercenaries, and so much more. Of course, Seagal tropes appear in both seasons. Elijah Kane is a Renaissance man – not only is he a cop but he also knows everything about swords and weapons. He plays guitar, he's a lady's man, a master in Aikido and other martial arts, and so much more. Kane knows everything because he has experienced everything. Forget thinking that a normal person can have a timeline like Kane's life. Kane isn't a normal person. He has been a part of every agency known to man which is why he is above any mortal person.

A positive part of Season One, the writers do a great job in splitting screen time up so that it isn't all focused on Seagal. Everyone on the team plays a part to keep the story moving. Kane plays a leader's role, but his teammates are fleshed out, making it a more enjoyable viewing experience. The characters are still likable and semi-believable with their own personal flaws and problems. The stunt work and practical effects are great (minus the added CGI fire). But, like anything good in *True Justice*, it all gets thrown out by the lousy story.

The first season's finale took a semi-enjoyable show and turned it into a typical Seagal film. The Russians want to kill Kane and his team. Why? Because the police are about to figure out something huge. Bigger than Seattle's problems. More like a United States of America nuclear problem. In the last episode, two of the members from Kane's team die from a Russian mercenary assassin group. Yes, you read that right. The episode ends on a cliffhanger with the mercs in the police station fighting with Kane's team. After the dust settles, everything is okay. Wait a minute, no it's not! The mercenary leader thought to be killed by Kane is actually alive! He drops grenades and blows up the station. It ends with a "To be continued," screen. Meh.

Season Two focuses on Kane while his team remains an afterthought. Except the rookie cop. With two of his team dead, and one quitting so he can focus on his family, Kane and the rookie continue on by resigning from the police force and going rogue. Season Two gets more in depth with Kane's background – he was military, then CIA, then undercover in the Seattle Police Department and now undercover for the CIA again. The only thing missing was Kane working for the Illuminati. Season Two adds nothing more than new faces to the series. It is over the top unbelievable. It asks more questions than it answers, all while stroking

Seagal's ego. Although his name isn't in the writing credits, Seagal must have had a huge influence on how his character was portrayed in the second season. It takes away everything Season One built up.

Season Two's main plot is all about the Russians wanting nuclear weapons. Or was it really the Russians? Was it corrupted individuals, the military, or the U.S. government? The viewer has to fill in the blanks like a terrible Mad Lib. The second season is filled with more invincible overweight sleuthing Seagal. His team is the best of the best, except when they get beaten up in each episode. Want to know what happened to the cop that quit to focus on his family? Instead of just writing him off as a retired cop, he gets killed by an assassin. More team members die, adding no value to the story. It becomes a "whodunnit" series. If *True Justice* could have finished properly, I'm convinced it would have been Elijah Kane that was behind it all.

Season Two does have a sleeker look to it. The camera work and acting was somewhat better, and the season seemed to have a bigger budget. It also had good stunt work, graphics, and practical effects (again, minus the added fire effects on explosions). Seagal even loses the weird accent he had in Season One. There could have been a lot of promise here. It's just too bad that the story was so awful.

What irks me the most about *True Justice* is Steven Seagal's invincibility throughout the show. He does not fail or falter. His teammates are human, but he is god-like. Out of the whole series, only twice did an antagonist get in a little offense on Seagal. Just once, I would have liked to have seen Seagal on the losing end. Other action heroes have their moments where all hope seems lost. Look at the many characters portrayed by Stallone, Schwarzenegger, and Van Damme. Seagal's character has none of the faults that we find endearing in other action stars. Elijah Kane is a child's interpretation of an action hero. He is too much in *True Justice*. A hero that has no weakness is not entertaining. Especially not for twenty-six episodes.

Overall, the series falls short. But if there is a record for most shootouts or bullets fired in a television series, I believe this one takes the prize. Seriously, almost all of the episodes had a shootout with magic guns and everlasting ammo. If this was turned into a drinking game, people would be hospitalized.

Would I recommend Seagal's *True Justice*? No. This series is for the die hard, completionist fan. The negatives far outweigh the positives. There were plenty of times where I asked myself, "Is it over yet?" There are many other similar movies and television shows that do a better job at telling a completed story. If they would have stuck with one format, I might be singing a different tune. But going from different formats and writing styles with an invincible lead character was nothing I ever wanted to see as an adult. As a matter of fact, I would consider this series as a false inequity.

–John Bruske

Force of Execution (2013)

"Holy shit?! Dave, what did I get myself into?" This phrase kept entering my ever-melting brain while watching the direct-to-video shit-fest that is *Force of Execution* (2013). Never heard of it? Of course, you haven't. Even among bad Seagal movies its considered bottom-of-the-barrel. But I agreed to do this, so I sucked it up. The following is partly a review and partly me spewing all my pain all over this page in retribution for having to not only sit through this nonsense but, craft a coherent stream of consciousness. I mean, the filmmakers didn't bother to do this.

The plot, of which there is, centers around underworld boss Alexander (Steven Seagal) with a "code of conduct". His top assassin, named Hurst (Bren Foster), is tasked with cosplaying as a prison guard. His mission is to kill an inmate named Benny (Cajardo Lindsey). Since nobody gave Hurst even a picture of the mark, he kills the wrong guy. Hurst shoots the incorrect inmate because a fellow inmate and kingpin named Ice Man (Ving Rhames), points out the wrong guy. Fucking really? Hurst (and not Ice Man?) is punished for his mistake by having his hand smashed in. Alexander orders that he be left alive because he likes him. Hurst goes from a well-dressed man about town to homeless in no time and is on a downward spiral. Meanwhile, Ice Man is out of jail and making moves to take over Alexander's enterprises in the underworld. For reasons of plot convenience, Hurst meets and saves a cook named Oso (Danny Trejo) and also meets a contrived love interest named Karen (Jenny Gabrielle). Karen also just happens to run a diner owned by Alexander for some reason. Oso repays Hurst for saving him by fixing his broken hand. With a renewed purpose Hurst joins Alexander and his men to help bring down Ice Man and his gang. It ends basically how you would expect: with lots of shooting, hacky martial arts, knife fights and a weirdly anti-climatic showdown between Ice and Alexander. I knew I was in for a long, hard ride, and, oh, brother, was I. Before pressing play on my rental (I actually paid 2 bucks to rent this thing), I told myself, maybe it won't be so bad. Maybe it will at least be so-bad-its-good, kind of like *The Room* (2003) or *Troll 2* (1990). I told myself this, but I knew in my heart that I was in a world of pain.

It was somehow worse than I thought. At least outings like *The Room* have some kind of endearing charm to them. Other films of this ilk take big swings that are ridiculous. While they fail, they at least feel sincere. *Force of Execution* is a loud, crass film that is so painfully inept yet very by-the-numbers. It languishes in this world of ultra-machismo, chocked full of sexism and cringe-worthy racist caricatures. For example, badass incarnate Danny Trejo plays a Mexican witch doctor (his own words, by the way) and, only exists in the film to fix the main characters broken hand with magic scorpions (again, you think I'm kidding, but, nope, that actually happens). For his trouble, the awesome character actor is killed. It's a shame because Trejo was probably the best thing in this film. Women serve as glorified set dressing, and, while I'm sure straight guys will love the strip club scenes, they were wasted on me.

The acting is exactly what you would expect for this dumpster fire of a film. I will say that Ving Rhames is, for me, a highlight. He is clearly having fun with this role, and like Trejo, he makes it just bearable. As for Seagal himself, well, I can only describe his performance as lazy. Maybe it's the fact that he's done so many of these but, he sleep walks through the entire affair. Clearly his action glory days are far behind him, and sadly, I think he knows it. It's like he doesn't have the energy for his own film, which is actually pretty sad. Worst of all, he mumbles and mush-mouths through a baffling Cajon accent. I'm not kidding when I say it's truly awful and it had me in tears. It's honestly so hard to understand him and I had to use subtitles to even begin to grasp what he was saying, not that the dialogue was important or anything. Strangely enough, the film takes itself far too seriously for its own good. Obviously, the filmmakers must have known this was nonsense, so why not at least go way over-the-top with it? When looking at the director's body-of-work, his output is largely straight-to-video, testosterone-fueled action films. While I haven't seen his other films, just going by some of the plot summaries they all seem very paint-by-number. These are the kind of films that pander to the lowest common audience. And listen, I'm not a movie snob. I certainly enjoy my share of trashy, low-brow fun, but damnit, it should be entertaining. This my friends, is far from that.

I originally wanted to do something more creative with this review, but I kept coming up short. I thought maybe I was the problem, but honestly, *Execution* is so devoid of anything remotely interesting and so riddled with plot holes that it was nearly impossible to make heads or tails of the whole thing. After watching the movie, which felt like three hours, I sat in silence for a while, I took my dog for a walk because I needed to clear what was left of my poor brain. Later, I watched a much better movie to get rid of the stink of Seagal's mumble garbage. I bitch, but I will say I don't regret being a part of this book project. David Hayes is a brilliant writer, author, actor and teacher, but how can I forgive him for torturing me with this mess of a movie? Maybe I should have watched *Back Woods* instead.

—Mike Vaughn

A *FORCE OF EXECUTION* SONNET BY MICHAEL VAUGHN

Thou underworld lord Alexander orders thy top assassin Hurst to execute Benny an imprisoned man.

As twisted fate thou have, Hurst slays the wrong man of the house of Dre. This trickery is by thou hand of the revival house of Ice.

For his misdeeds Hurst is punished by Lord Alexander's man Dante and has thoust hand mangled. He is cast out of his clan.

Lord Alexander weeps in his heart and gives Hurst coins to sustain thou-self. Meanwhile in a house of vice, Ice plots to overthrow Lord Alexander

Lord Ice gifts the House of Alexander with thou gift of Dre, the rogue man Hurst was supposed to slay.

In thy bid to over throw Lord Alexander, Ice makes traitorous dealings with Lord Alexanders allies with haste

Constantine, thou top clan member is killed, leaving Lord Alexander in peril. Downth Alexander cannot lay.

Lord Ice's men kidnaps fair maiden from a local tavern named Karen. With brutish force and grumble her virtue they do they do try and taste.

Lord Alexander's ally Hurst befriends a mysterious witch-doctor who thou using scorpion magik dost thou save his crippled hand.

Lord Alexander meets Ice in a house of ill repute and villainy. weary of fighting Alexander and thou offer Ice a truce with the promise that thou will flee and hand over power. Ice agrees but plans an traitorous act.

Both houses suit up for battle armed with bow, arrow, knives the eastern art of self-preservation. Erstwhile Alexanders man Dante is slaughtered. The honorable Hurst find out where the maiden Karen and Ice's men. His victory is thou to be grand.

Lord Ice and his men storm Lord Alexander and his army. Many bodies do fall in the grisly battle. When all thou souls are silenced Alexander and Hourst have a final stand with Ice. Ice wanting to flee begs Lord Alexander to show him the outdoor entrance. Lord Alexander in a bold and hearty manner quips "You Die" then shoots ice whose body does sack.

Haven won the day Lord Alexander laments that he is a dinosaur, living amongst men. Thou wants to retire and live out his glory days in peace.

Though he regrets things he has done, with a coy smile he exclaims he doesn't regret everything.

His killing he dost thou wish to cease.

A Good Man (2014)

Alexander, played by Steven Seagal, is an ex special forces guy who just so happens to be a good handyman neighbor. Unfortunately, unlike a good neighbor who should be there, Seagal isn't. Or is, but only barely.

The film opens with Seagal and his special forces team closing in on a target code named Abdul Normal (pause for uproarious laughter) Seagal inexplicably speaks like a 15-year-old street thug and his movements are rigid as hell. His face looks simultaneously bloated and Botoxed and the dye in his goatee and hair are at extreme odds with his obvious age.

The first few minutes cut between the title credits, some hokey narration by Seagal about how he has both light and darkness within himself, and some slow motion staring into an explosion for no apparent reason. Maybe the slow motion staring is to signal to the viewer what to expect from Seagal in this film, which is not much and what there is of him is slow moving.

Whomever is commanding the special forces decides to blow the whole compound up despite Seagal's repeated warning that there are women and children in the base being used as human shields. Seagal manages to shoot Abdul before a drone strike levels the place. A secondary target, a Chinese arms dealer named Mr. Chen escapes and just before the bomb explodes. Seagal tries to rescue a little girl but is unsuccessful. The child dies in the blast.

Two years later in Europe Seagal is suddenly blessed with the ability to speak in complete sentences. He befriends Lena and her small sister Mya (who of course reminds Alexander of the girl he tried to save at the beginning of the flick) live next door in his apartment building. This unfolds in 10 minutes or less in the film and then Seagal vanishes. The narrative switches to the cliched bad guy nightclub/stripper/lap dance joint where Lena is forced to work as a bartender for the Russian mob because her dad owed the mob money and was killed or died before paying it back. The debt then fell on Lena's shoulders to pay. Thank goodness she has a half-brother named Sasha who's ex-military and comes to help bail her out by working for the mob!

Sasha played by Victor Webster becomes the focus of the kung-fu-ery in *A Good Man*. He's actually the protagonist but Seagal is inserted into the works every so often to flip somebody over a glass coffee table or stab somebody in the neck six or eight times.

It's no surprise that Mr. Chen is doing business with the Russian mob. Seagal fixes it where he kills some guys threatening Lena and then makes it look like the Russian mob is doing it and trying to steal from Chen. Lots and lots of time is used setting up the Russian mob and Chen and their association. We even have some obligatory cops who follow along so that the plot can be explained to those viewers with less brain power than a starfish. Well, I suppose if you're watching these sorts of films, you're probably not in the over achiever's section…anyways, moving along…

Eventually, Mya is given to Mr. Chen in lieu of money owed to him. Chen wastes no time in delivering the girl to his customer who is (conveniently) a pedophile. When that happens, Alexander and Sasha team up to bring Mya home and mercifully bring this direct to video disaster to a close.

The end of A Good Man is the opposite of epic. Its hilarious. Alexander and Mr. Chen have a sword fight to the death. Everyone else brought guns. The Russian mob brought guns, Chen's guys brought guns, hell even Chen himself had a gun that he was going to shoot the kid with. However, after a headache inducing speech where Alexander challenges Chen to look at his entire life and examine if he wants to die under the weight of killing an innocent child, Chen contemplates for a moment and decides he doesn't. Would it be ok though if he died in a sword fight rather than a gunfight? Alexander ponders this weighty request and then nods his approval.

I won't say how it ends, though. I wouldn't want to ruin the ending.

Stunning highlights of idiocy in this film include a love scene between Alexander and Lena where Seagal doesn't even remove his black leather coat. Or pants. Or shoes I'm assuming. Lena, who is young enough to be his granddaughter either doesn't notice he's fully dressed or is just so enamored with him she doesn't care, a scene where two adversaries throw their guns on the floor , fight hand to hand, hand to knife, and pipe to pipe when just shooting at each other would have saved several minutes of bad fight choreography. In yet another scene two men brandishing guns drag a minor character who knows the entire plot over to a junked-out car, handcuffs this person to the car and then lights the car on fire. Did I mention that the men doing this were carrying guns so why….? Never mind.

Seagal isn't actually in a lot of the film. It should have said "guest appearance by Steven Seagal". When he is on screen his dialogue is flat, like he's practicing the line in front of a mirror. His eyes are expressionless little beads embedded in big pillows of skin. I've seen totem poles with more range!

The directing and editing leave a lot to be desired. Scenes begin with the narrative in progress. Many times I had a distinct feeling that I missed a minute or two of important dialogue or action that may explain how suddenly a character is here or there or why time has suddenly jumped forward. The script was nonsensical in many places, but it was by far the least this movie had to worry about.

I can sum my experience up now by quoting a character from the film.

"I can now die in peace".

He may have been a good man, but he was in a terrible, terrible movie.

–Charles E. Pratt, Jr.

Gutshot Straight (2014)

This gem of a movie starts good enough to be a guilty pleasure. When it starts, we see that Jack (George Eads) needs help from Paulie (Seagal), and then we are treated to a title sequence that is up there with the James Bond quality featuring cutaways of beautiful women and playing cards. As much as I wanted to just tear this movie to shreds in terms of some sort of quality, be it, acting, directing, writing, I'm even willing to attack cinematography, this film did above average. I was impressed with the first few scenes, and honestly, I found myself asking, "When is this movie going to suck?"

Here's where it went right. Seagal is not the hero of the film. He's also not even the main antagonist, and this almost plays like a Guy Ritchie film with the ensemble approach. The story is also above the rest of the traditional Seagal fare we have been getting in recent years. It goes against the grain of making it a good guy versus bad guy approach that almost all of his other films go to and approaches it as a noir thriller. If you look at how *IMDB* classifies it as a movie, it's a crime thriller, there is hardly any action in the movie at all, and when it is, it's quick and to the point, which is a nice change of pace as well. I don't recall Seagal doing any martial arts in the movie at all, he gives Eads the tools to do the job and then sits back and watches, until he is called upon on again.

I mention the story is above the rest, so here is the plot, Jack is a gambler with a streak of bad luck, he meets Duffy, a shady individual with eccentric behavior. After a fun night on the Vegas strip, Duffy invites Jack back to his house. He meets May, the beautiful woman of the house. Duffy offers to pay money to see Jack sleep with May. Jack says no, and a fight erupts. Duffy is accidentally killed, and instead of calling the police, Jack and May decide to get rid of the body, except their actions are caught on camera. It's nice to have a plot that is different than "Seagal plays a (insert law enforcement type officer here) when a terrorist organization from (insert foreign country here) kidnaps or murders a (insert a type of hostage here)" cookie- cutter plot outline.

It's nice when we have a real story and spend time with the characters. You aren't getting sensory overload with all the gunfire and action sequences; you are caring about the characters. Eads plays Jack with such a likability; you are afraid for him, and yet you do see that he is doing dumb shit. Ted Levine, who plays Duffy's brother, is as always, a great villain. The first scene between Lewis and Jack is a great lesson in creating tension. It doesn't go anywhere for a little bit of time. It enjoys just simmering right below the surface. Steven Seagal actually turns in one of his better performances by playing a crime boss. Sometimes if you close your eyes, you can honestly hear him try to channel Marlon Brando. He is only in three or four scenes, but they are vital. I almost hope he considers doing more ensemble work; he works better in his older age when he is not the focus of the movie. He is seen bigger on the poster as well as Vinnie Jones, but it's George Eads' movie, and it's better off for it.

The script follows the traditional beats of noir. It's nice to have a dialogue where it's more than characters trying to one-up another; there just seems to be more intelligence to the writing. I can't decide if it's actual intelligence or I have just been suffering through a slew of Seagal films, that anything that doesn't sound like something a college student who watches too many movies, would type into a screenwriting program for a college short, is Shakespeare by comparison.

The cinematography does take a hit. There is a flux of quality of the images on the screen. Sometimes it's beautiful and reminds me of those blue-tinted movies with the perfect mysterious look that noir requires, with the crystal-clear image. Scenes that take place in broad daylight look like the producers gave a DSLR camera and tripod to an intern and said point it at Eads. some quick insert shots look like they were shot with a handheld camera that is not designed for film, but more of a still image camera, that has a recording function. There are sometimes if that was just a stylistic choice from the director or if it was one of the joys of working on a low-budget film.

The story does seem to borrow from several movies where tropes are done better. You got a femme fatal, so on the nose in certain scenes, I was half expecting her to drop 1930s jargon. You have a villain who will resort to hurting children to get his way. The most expected ending comes about when Jack realizes that he can turn the two men who want him dead, against each other.

As I stated earlier, I wanted to know when this movie was going to suck. It never actually did. I was focused on the story, and I liked the twists and turns on things. It goes go into predictable territory more than I would have preferred; however, it's a different style of project for most of the cast that's involved, except for Ted Levine, who has done every genre imaginable. I think this went direct to video for its runtime, which is a quick 85 minutes. It also has some lower quality scenes in terms of lighting; however, after the recent crap Seagal was doing, this was a wonderful change of pace.

–Stephen Kessen

Mercenary: Absolution (2015)

Mercenary: Absolution opens with scenes reminiscent of a torture porn flick, intercut with Seagal's narration about needing (bum bum bum!) *Absolution* for the bad things his character John Alexander has done in life as a contract killer.

We meet his handler, Van Horn (Howard Dell). Forget subtle foreshadowing, Alexander threatens him right off, so we know it's going to end bad for this guy.

Concerning his latest target, we're treated with such dialog as "If it turns out that he's really a bad guy and he's really an enemy of the United States [of] America or he's really funding terrorist activities or any of those things, I'll make him disappear" which makes you wonder how much leeway co-writer/director Keoni Waxman gave Seagal to improvise because surely that near-legal jargon of conditional clauses can't have been in the script, or maybe that's just the kind of discriminating hitman Alexander is. A few other lines sound improvised, but really, who's going to tell Seagal to can the exposition?

Next, we meet Alexander's brother-in-arms, Chi (Byron Mann). One thing that perhaps sets this apart from other Seagal films is that Chi is a capable fighter and nearly equal partner (Never show up Seagal!). You're expecting him to die at any moment just to give Alexander further motivation to kill somebody, as if ever really needed.

An unnecessary addition to the film are the speechless flashbacks of a woman *IMDB* credits as "John's Wife" (Sabina Branduse), but considering how young she appears I would have appreciated a younger Seagal lookalike or at least a shaven Seagal with a girdle on so not to look more like a concerned father.

The monkey wrench in Alexander and Chi's plan (also the plot) occurs when a victim of the masked sadist (both seen earlier) escapes with his video camera containing footage of his exploits and his exposed face. Nadia (Adina Stetcu) runs into the bar where the hitmen are awaiting their extraction. They take on the baddies following her and though they try to ditch her afterwards, Alexander breaks protocol and gets involved in her plight.

To facilitate their escape and navigate the city until help arrives, Alexander contacts Sergei (Cosmin Dominte). We learn of the Syndicate, which neither Chi nor Sergei, who we thought were men of the street, knows about. Now I've never been a career criminal, but I know a syndicate is pretty much the mafia. Shouldn't your average "man on the street" know there's one in every metropolis? When Chi asks, "What is the Syndicate?" Sergei informs him he'll check his sources. Wouldn't a more fitting question be "Who RUNS the Syndicate?"

Another winning moment of dialog:

Sergei: "This used to be a safe city."

Chi: "When?"

Sergei: "Before all this."

I suppose we have to forgive Sergei as English isn't his primary language.

We get another flashback, now of Alexander's wife in bed, dying of cancer I suppose.

Absolution's sole claim to fame might be that it has to feature the slowest and least dramatic car chase in cinematic history. This occurs right after Alexander detonates a bomb via remote, sending the flaming victim through a hotel room window and down several stories onto a car. Alexander peels out in reverse and turns down a road. The victim's partner gets in his Jeep and does likewise, only when they get on the highway they're both driving a respectable speed as everyone else (35mph?).

Alexander manages to make a left at a median and loses the guy. That's it. Alexander and Nadia arrive at their destination safely without a single vehicular accident or honked horn in their wake. The chase is over in less than a minute and we never see the other car catch up, so we're unsure at what point the driver gave up such a high-stakes pursuit.

An hour in we finally discover the head of the Syndicate is The Boss. No kidding. Played by Vinnie Jones, it's a good thing Chi doesn't ask "Who's the boss?" or else we'd have to wait another hour for Sergei to check his sources again.

Nadia has to find her video camera at the club, where Alexander takes on a few baddies, including a beautifully bearded *Samurai Cop*-era Robert Z'Dar lookalike (or two), while Chi takes on a Jean Claude Van Damme clone. Having died in the melee, Sergei is avenged with a butterfly knife to JCVD Part 2's throat.

Van Horn, now with the Boss as they give Chi a beat down, telephones Alexander, who replies "There's a big difference between a real warrior and a wannabe. Wannabes are always talking … Real warriors they don't really say much," but then goes on to converse another minute. Alexander claims to have foreseen the event and implies it was part of his plan, yet nothing that follows has any appearance of strategy.

The movie's best kill is the Popeye/Bluto-esque move Alexander employs, stepping on a baddie's foot and using him as a punching bag before breaking his arm followed with a nice two-finger throat jab.

As usual in Seagal films no one can lay a hand on him, not even the final boss, aka The Boss. Tradition in videogames and action movies is that the final boss presents the greatest challenge. We want the whole Rocky arc in the last five-minute battle. We want to see the hero pushed to his limits, beaten down, and rise like the Phoenix victorious. Never with Seagal. He might get shot because he's human and can't block bullets, but never will a finger touch him.

Chi takes quite the beating, understandably since he's been hit by a car and shot by now, but he still comes out in one piece.

The story closes with Seagal's narration of starting over and a look at his new life with Nadia before we cut to a smiling Chi coming from the massage parlor. Really, what more can you ask from a Seagal movie than a happy ending?

–A P Sessler

Sniper Special Ops (2016)

As an American, starting a movie like *Sniper Special Ops* brings some expectation with it. The American military has long held an almost mythological sense of power, and special forces operators are elevated to an even greater level.

Still, if there's one thing us beer-drinking, American-flag-tank-top-wearing patriots love more than anything else?

It's the sniper.

I've often wondered if it's our cultural fascination with guns in general, or maybe it's tied to the fact that we are a very individualistic culture. In movies, the sniper often works alone or with a "subordinate," a spotter, obviously less important because he's holding binoculars, not a gun. We essentially have this solitary gunman with the ability to kill someone from so far away that the sniper is untouchable. Immortal. The real stories of snipers taking out their targets from miles away are impressive enough, but in Hollywood's hands?

They become gods.

There are rules, though. First, everyone knows that snipers use the big rifles. Long barrels, massive scopes. Second, they save the lives of their compatriots in the field with last-second timing to build tension. Third, don't even get me started on silencers and thermal scopes. They're like icing on this mythological cake.

So with a title like *Sniper Special Ops*, it feels like we can sit down with Steven Seagal and friends and we know what we're getting into.

And *Sniper Special Ops* starts out strong! The very first scene gives us everything we want in an exciting film about a sniper. We've got a special ops team moving into a war-torn village in the desert. There's witty banter and snappy repartee from the troops. We've got large men in desert camo weaving through a village, while Chandler (Seagal) and his spotter watch from 550 - 650 meters away to cover their advance.

And twelve-point-five minutes into this film, he abandons that sweet, silenced, long-range dealer of death and as far as I could tell he didn't pick it up again for the entire movie. He stands up, grabs an assault rifle, and proceeds to spray bullets from the rooftop. From 550 - 650 meters away.

This really sets the tone for the rest of the movie.

Except the part about him standing up.

Disbelief can only be suspended so far. The firefights play out like an online game of Modern Warfare. Special Operatives leaving cover to pause in the wide-open might be great for looking powerful on camera, but it doesn't take long to realize that if you wait to see who abandons their cover, you can guess who is going to get shot next.

My friend decided to take a shot of whiskey every time Vazquez (played by Rob Van Dam) would hold his gun up to his face, then close the eye that should be aiming down the sights. I need to check on my buddy; I haven't heard from him since about halfway through the film.

And then there's Janet (Charlene Amoia), a journalist who just so happens to also be an expert marksman. And I mean expert. In a later firefight, when the spec ops team is pinned down, she uses a pistol one of the other soldiers gave her "just in case" and manages to wipe out the enemy force with it. I can't stop wondering why she wasn't written in as...a soldier? Is it more believable that a journalist could be a ninja-astronaut-cowboy than it is that a woman could be part of a special forces unit in the military?

Then you could also cut out the part where she's smiling as she takes pictures of dead bodies. Yeah, that was probably a slip in the filming, but it was still weird.

So yes--Chandler and his spotter, Cannon (played by Daniel Booko, whose dad went to high school with my mom, I think? What a small world) are left behind and nobody ever gets left behind, right? That's our basic source of tension.

And the sniper team sits, and they wait. Chandler is shown to be "saving the cat" by staying behind with his spotter, so that's why we like him... right? I mean, Cannon has to sit because he can't feel his legs anymore, so that I get. But Chandler sits, until he gets thirsty, so he goes to get water. Then there's more sitting and waiting. Some backstory is given... while they sit. The music does get a little bit tense. Tense-sitting-music is the biggest danger the left-behind sniper and his now-paralyzed spotter are under. Considering this guy is essentially the title of the movie, his character is absolutely lethargic.

On the Spec Ops side, things are more interesting. There's some business about a convoy, and a detour. Commands from "the brass" are given; commands from "The brass" are broken. There's more shooting. It's tough to avoid spoilers while telling you about my favorite part of the movie--where Janet trades a granola bar for a baby they find in the back of a truck.

Oops, I probably just spoiled it.

But Chandler does come back to save the day! In the final shootout, I don't think anybody except him hits a gosh-darned thing, though guns are firing everywhere, and the air is filled with hot brass. No, he stands on his rooftop, spraying bullets from his assault rifle (I really feel cheated that he's not using that amazing sniper rifle--where did it go?) and killing every enemy who runs into the wide-open middle of the street. There are also explosions.

The only performance I really enjoyed was from the Spec Ops commander, Vic (Tim Abell). Maybe it sounded like he was making up gibberish words in the very beginning as he was chatting on the radio, but by the end, he was at least worth rooting for.

It's too bad he wasn't an executive producer. Maybe then, he could have been given the obviously-rented sniper rifle for the first 12.5 minutes of the movie before sitting around for the rest of the production.

–Christopher Smith

Code of Honor (2016)

Unlike *Ticker,* which was far worse than I expected, it's fair to say that *Code of Honor* was far better than I expected, albeit better despite Steven Seagal's involvement rather than because of it.

Initially, it seems to be all about him and it's unintentionally comical. He's on top of a giant silo looking like Fidel Castro, especially as his first action is to cut and light a cigar, in profile. He's almost hidden behind rose-tinted sunglasses, a backwards baseball cap and a bulky scarf, not to forget a bulkier jacket, so it's only his patented facial hair that identifies him as Steven Seagal. Nobody can see him up there, but he's deliberately hiding every inch of his skin anyway. How many chins does he have under there? He also alternates between phallic symbols: playing with his cigar, playing with his gun, playing with his cigar, playing with his gun...

Down below is a gangland deal, with lots of money, lots of drugs and lots of very bad guys. Seagal starts killing the latter with his sniper rifle, his automatic rifle, whatever his other rifle is. Then he triggers a bomb under a car and realises that not everybody's dead, so he abseils down the silo to knife another gangbanger to death. He leaves the coke and the money with the corpses and, amazingly, it's still there when the cops look at the scene.

A blink of an eye later, he blows up the Snake Eyes strip club. Then he shoots a couple of crooks in the process of being handcuffed by the cops, which, let's face it, is about as ballsy as it gets. He targets pimps, drug dealers, the scum of the city, who may or may not all work in some way for Vincent Romano, the local kingpin.

James Russo plays Romano like a cartoon, emerging under special red lighting with just the right devilish tint. He doesn't so much act this part as pose it and always outrageously. Seagal's a cartoon too but he doesn't have the energy to pose and he's only a year older. Russo relishes in the poses. Without them, Romano would cease to be.

Clearly Seagal is a vigilante but he doesn't have a manifesto and he doesn't send notes to the press. We'd know nothing at all about him except that he has Special Agent William Porter as his carnival barker. Porter shows up unofficially and sells him something rotten to the local police department. The vigilante is Colonel Robert Sikes, he says, the former commander of one of the most elite special forces units. He's an expert in guns, bombs, everything. He's a talented chameleon. He can leap small buildings with a single bound. He's like Chuck Norris in all the memes. And he always leaves one witness, to spread fear. Except when he doesn't.

We're happy for Porter because actor Craig Sheffer is a lot more grounded than Seagal and Porter's ongoing attempts to track and stop Sikes are action packed, especially when he's saving the life of Keri Green, the stripper who perhaps saw Sikes at Snake Eyes. He's up against it, it seems, even though he's crazy talented too. He gets a great scene where he's one side of a gunfight in Romano's flagship club, but he can't leave his chair because Sikes has armed a bomb underneath it. In fact, he's so tough that he can hammer a clip into a pistol with a palm that he's just been shot through and which is still bleeding through its bandage, without even blinking. That's tough.

In fact, the film moves along nicely with characters like Porter and Keri and her six-year-old son; Detective Peterson and Captain Connely; Romano and his thugs; sleazy journalist Jerry Simon of *Jerry Simon Says*; creepy old Mayor Randolf and his neverending supply of sweet young things… it's almost like there's an actual plot that these characters want to work their way through and we want to watch them. I wasn't expecting that from a 2016 Steven Seagal movie.

What I was expecting is what I get from Seagal. He doesn't interact with anyone else in the picture except Porter and the lowlifes he kills. He doesn't open his mouth until 45 minutes into the picture and, when he does, it's to rationalise his deeds in an inexplicable mild Cajun accent.

Slavery was a law, he says, so defending the country means that he has to ignore laws, which in turn means that it's not merely OK, it's his actual sworn duty to murder lots of people.

This is latter day bloated Seagal, so he doesn't move much either and, frankly, it doesn't look like he can. When he does move, he sort of floats forward like he's a Steven Seagal shaped Dalek, plungers waving around with knives in them. Occasionally, the scene shifts into near silhouette so a much slimmer body double can move on his behalf, before jumping back to him in close-up.

Apparently aware of these limitations, he's content for the most part with killing from a distance with his sniper rifle. He nails one particular headshot from such a ridiculous distance that there's no way that you would believe me if I even told you. I'm doubtful that Superman could see that far and Porter wouldn't have talked his talents up quite so emphatically.

I'm being careful not to spoil this movie because the twist, while hardly unprecedented, is capably handled. There's foreshadowing when needed and I've littered hints throughout this review too, but it doesn't become obvious until late on, albeit before the script hammers it home just to be sure, and I appreciated that. There's even a slight twist on the twist.

I can't say that this will prod me towards more recent Steven Seagal movies, but it may well prod me towards more films made by writer/ director Michael Winnick. I'd only seen one before this—*Guns, Girls and Gambling*—and I enjoyed that too.

–Hal CF Astell

1000 Hands of the Guru (2016)

I am a sucker for a good documentary. This is an unusual case as I usually critique Seagal's acting or writing or directing. With this film, he plays himself as he is interviewed about Buddhist art, which is a welcomed break from the poor production values of his normal direct-to video-fare. The total runtime comes to 66 minutes with Seagal's screen time probably around one minute wherein he just answers a couple of questions. He is not the focus of this documentary by a long shot. It's more focused on the monks and the art preservationists. In all honesty, I think his name was added for clout and to get interest in the film which, in turn, makes this is one of the better films Seagal has lent his name to.

You can tell this film was made with passion and the utmost respect for Buddha. It focuses on one spectacular work of art, a painted scroll depicting, you guessed it, 1000 hands coming out from all around the central figure. It's also about the dying art of scroll preservation like that, when the monks would rather create new ones with a very interesting look at the craft itself.

It also depicts the "invasion of the screen," meaning the use of digital technology like phones when it comes to storytelling and how stories used to pass down through generations. It is odd to see a traditional monk look at a cell phone, but they are in the 21st Century as well.

This film is perfect for art lovers, religious scholars, and anyone who wants to watch something light and learned with the family. I never thought I would see a movie with Steven Seagal have a G-rating, but here we are. Even though his screen time is limited, he is passionate and the paintings from his private collection are beautiful. It would appear that one of Hollywood's most notorious ass-kickers has a soft side and collects incredibly beautiful art. The narrative does delve into PBS documentary territory, so be prepared for that, but after all the violence I have watched, this was a welcomed change of pace.

The Buddhist life and works of art are the real stars of the film. Everything they design, not just the scrolls, things like surf boards and more are beautiful. They are covered with color and more importantly tell a story of some kind. We are treated to some of the most unique underwater footage during this portion of the documentary. We also get some time lapse of them working on their art which really conveys the width and breadth of the process. We are treated to an explanation of how the artists feel when they paint and that it's a spiritual connection and how they devote so much of their life, story, culture and faith into their paintings. Nice to see a group of people peacefully creating away from the hustle and bustle of normal life.

In terms of the actual documentary, I love the approach. It feels like real time as opposed to a look back, so you see subjects doing things for the first time as opposed to being in a room reflecting on what they did or what they witnessed. Culture is up close and it is beautiful. I know this film will be a tough pill to swallow, as it is about a niche subject, but it is gorgeous. There are times where it feels less like a film for entertainment and more of a film made to promote something. I'm not saying its propaganda, but it's definitely a film that would be made by a company or maybe a group of volunteers trying to raise money for a cause. I did appreciate the use of metrics to explain the dedication it takes with my favorite one saying that each piece would take between 3-7 months to restore. Considering how many pieces the monks have to restore, it would take over 300,000 years to complete everything. A number like that really puts into perspective the reason why artists would want to create more than spend the intensive time to restore something.

This film is a true passion project from everyone involved. Normally, I would give my personal take on Seagal's performance, but with films like this, it's no way fair. I know he was just being interviewed and this he was on camera as himself, but this is one of the more entertaining and informative films Seagal has done.

–Stephen Kessen

Asian Connection (2016)

BYRON GIBSON

PIM BUBEAR – JOHN EDWARD LEE

STEVEN SEAGAL

Sahnjak BOONTHANAKIT–JohnEdw. LEE

YOU'VE BEEN SHOT, JACK!
YEAH, NO SHIT! BUT THAT ARMORED SEMI PASSING US IS SIRINKIRI. HE SAW ME!
JOHN EDWARD LEE - PIM BUBEAR
SSKREE!!
ARMORED SEMIS-R-US
TURN THIS MOTHER-FUCKIN' TRUCK AROUND!
STEVEN SEAGAL
YOU KILLED HIM!
FUCKIN' A! NOW LEAVE THE MONEY & HIT THE BRICKS.
WHY ARE YOU LETTING ME GO?
J.E.LEE - S. SEAGAL - P. BUBEAR
COZ I CARE. COZ I'M ONE OF THE GOOD DRUG LORDS! (IT'S ALSO WHY I DRESS LIKE A PIRATE. ARRRR.) NOW RUN BEFORE I CHANGE MY MIND, BITCH.
END
STEVEN SEAGAL

The Perfect Weapon (2016)

The Prefect Weapon stars Johnny Messner, Sasha Jackson, and Steven Seagal in a futuristic action flick. In the not-so-distant future, the world has suffered and unknown event that threatened society. In an effort to save that society, "The State," under the leadership of The Director (Seagal), has taken over. They use a combination of constant surveillance and hitmen to control the populace, but one of those hitmen seems to have grown a conscience.

We see this surveillance in full effect in the opening sequence as it shows information about everyone we see with what looks like an overlay created in 1984 by a 12 year old with only a cursory understanding of what a computer screen looks like. We also see giant screens all over the city constantly playing the State-run news and a video of what looks like a Steven Seagal that just ate another Steven Seagal. The sequence ends with the surveillance on one person showing that that person cannot be read. This is our hero, Condor (Messner).

We follow Condor to a tea house where he is served without ordering, which turns out to be a dead drop. The drop is some form of Japanese-inspired piece of paper. It seems important to Condor, so I just assumed that is what was happening. To this point, Condor has yet to speak either in monologue or to anyone else. The State-run media playing on a nearby TV is interrupted by a "pirate broadcast." We know it is a pirate broadcast because it literally says so in the upper right. This again appears important to Condor and he leaves.

Condor is on-mission now. He is hunting the speaker from the pirate broadcast, who we see enjoying a performance by a Geisha with two friends, speaking openly about their plans to overthrow "The State" in a world where every action and word is monitored by that same organization, seems smart. Condor appears for the first instance of coitus-interruptus and kills everyone except the Geisha, who seems to cause him some form of painful flashback.

Condor is called before The Controller, who happens to be the creepy dad from Kindergarten Cop, to be scolded for leaving someone alive when all witnesses were to be eliminated. For this failure, Condor is going to be sent to meet The Director and be "re-programmed". Condor begins pleading with The Controller, as it appears Condor thinks they are friends. While apparently going in peacefully, Condor attempts to escape using the Controller as a human shield. However, as he runs away from the men who cannot hit a man from three feet away with fully automatic weapons, he is shot by an unseen person in white with a tranquilizer facilitating his capture.

A conversation between The Controller and The Director, sees The Director looking to have this failing asset eliminated, but The Controller insists that Condor can be reprogrammed into The Perfect Weapon. That reprogramming fails miserably and Condor escapes. During the escape, where the Perfect Weapon gets his ass kicked repeatedly (you'd think the "Perfect Weapon" would be a better fighter) he stumbles across a woman in a cell that happens to be the woman he loved that he believed to be dead. She uses an instant heal wand to clean up his potentially fatal wound (the security cameras even show that his status is "dying" at one point) in an instant. They are finally able to escape using bulletproof cardboard boxes, henchmen with no ability to hit a target 5 feet in front of them with fully automatic weapons, and a delivery truck.

They decide the best way to evade a group that can see and hear everything is to go right back to Condor's apartment. They assume The State will be waiting for them, but once they enter the apartment and find no one there, they assume it is safe to just chill there for hours, taking showers and of course having sex, while waiting for the morning rush. Obviously, The State shows up for coitus-interruptus and Condor and his girl, Nina, are caught once again.

Condor is being tortured for the world to see what happens to traitors, when The Controller shows up to finish him off. What?!?! He is not there to kill him and saves him? This is madness. Condor and Nina find out that The Controller is working with a resistance group looking to overthrow The State and has a plan involving The Director's girlfriend who is absolutely loyal to him due to Stockholm Syndrome. The Director beats Condor and shows him that Nina and The Controller were in cahoots via a mirror/TV. It was all al lie, the love, the friendship, everything. It was all planted by The Controller to manipulate Condor into killing The Director so The Controller could take over. When Nina sees Condor, she kills The Controller to show Condor she had begun to love him, but Condor is not buying it and shoots her in the throat.

Condor returns to The Director who offers him The Controller job. Condor refuses it and stabs The Director then leaves him to bleed out. Once Condor leaves, we see ANOTHER Director appear to thank his "brother" for serving him so well and gives him an honorable death via a nearby katana setting up the inevitable sequel!

This movie was painful to watch. The plot is scatter shot, and the cinematography is awful with odd filters and appears that is was shot in the wrong aspect and then resized badly, so everything looks vertically compressed. I would also be remiss to not mention that I would assume Mr. Seagal had complete creative control over his character. The cultural appropriation is strong. From his wardrobe, to the decorations of his living space, even his Japanese girlfriend, everything had to have Japanese overtones. The only redeeming quality of this movie is that Condor has good taste in microwaves, he had the same one I have in my own home.

–Pat Kawula

End of a Gun (2016)

"If it's all about the money, you'll find yourself at the end of a gun," is the last line of the 2016 Steven Seagal film, *End of a Gun*. This is simplistic dialogue that has just as much purpose in a fortune cookie as a film script, and quite possibly a forewarning to Mr. Seagal himself. All actors, writers, filmmakers and artists, in general, create works that are clearly defined by the need for a paycheck, if many of these works are made for that sole purpose then the level of talent and security can become dangerously lacking. Now, while getting paid for work you've done is a necessity for everyone, without passion the work can become monotonous and tiresome. Passion is something I saw from Mr. Seagal's early work, but unfortunately, it is all too absent in this more recent endeavor.

With that said, I don't want to dismiss the film entirely, nor do I want to downplay the contributions made by Mr. Seagal over the past 32 years. There's a reason he has been able to make films on a continual basis since 1988's, *Above the Law,* and that's because he can still draw eyes to the screen with the promise of strong action scenes, trademark martial arts performances, the comfort of the classic motif of good triumphing over evil and a man's honor. Sadly, these four Steven Seagal staples were not very present in *End of a Gun*. These constructs were present but in a different way, though not what I am accustomed to in Mr. Seagal's previous work.

The film starts off like many low budget films designed to attract a young, male audience: quick cuts of highly sexualized women, a pulsating soundtrack, and the easy dispatch of an armed assailant manhandling a young woman. It's quick, simple, and sets the stage for the classic good vs. evil storyline. However, it then changes direction to become a confusing, tepid story that leaves the viewers to question the intent of main character Decker, played by Seagal himself. We are left to wonder if honor is a word he truly knows the meaning of, or has it become one more thing for him to pontificate about. Is it really about the honor when Decker attacks and subdues the young police officers unknowingly guarding the money that he seeks? Is it about the honor when lecherous Decker turns down the affection of his young co-star only to bed her minutes later? And, is it about the honor when an unscrupulous Decker apparently forgets about all the years spent in the DEA when he decides to retire to the Florida Keys once he secures said money? With these inconsistencies in character development, along with numerous style changes it's difficult to keep interested in the movie for any length of time, let alone 86 minutes.

As the film progresses, we are treated to a variety of film looks seen over the years, but never all in just one film. Seagal's Chinatown-esque voiceover narration is sprinkled throughout the film (all comparisons to *Chinatown* stop here), but never to a level that moves the story forward in any cohesive or interesting way. For some reason everyone's first language is English even though there seem to be four different characters with four different nationalities throughout the film, and it's set in Paris, France. So, I guess the French don't even speak French. Then, there is the lone Asian character that is set up to be a possible force to be reckoned initially but ends up being the short-lived comic relief. I'm just not sure why he was there. The multiscreen montage brings us back to the look of the sixties only to end up with the television style editing of a *CSI*. Granted, the CSI style editing is television trying to be more film-like and not vice-versa, but the dissociative identity disorder of the film does nothing to enhance any quasi entertainment one might hope to extract from it.

However, this style of storytelling may explain some of Mr. Seagal's acting choices, and his own disassociation from the story and his character throughout the film. From the beginning, he played his character with a part hippie, part urban "philosopher" style that kind of reminds you of the Seagal of yester-year, but doesn't quite make it. Again, he talks about honor, but then turns around almost immediately and shoots honor in the back of the head. Now, it could be that Mr. Seagal decided to use this film to expand his acting abilities and try styles, dialects, and choices he might not normally partake in, but I would have preferred that he pick just one and stick with it.

As the film rolls along, I try to look for the positives – attractive co-star, Jade Ewen, Paris, employment for cast and crew – to salvage my once fascination with his movies and remember the good ol' days. Growing up as a suburban white kid, Steven Seagal seemed like a 1980's version of Bruce Lee; quick, powerful, righteous. That's a little hyperbole, but not much. His fight scenes were fun to watch, he had a good screen presence, and it's always nice to see the bad guys get their comeuppance. I was 17 when Seagal's first film, *Above the Law,* came out so suspending my disbelief wasn't a laborious chore and allowed me a few hours of entertainment that my mind could pass off as reality, at least in somebody's world. Did I mention I was seventeen? Unfortunately, not even the ignorance of adolescence could save this film from rotting tomatoes and the confused look on my face as I watched in horror the eighty-six minutes of my life slip away. Again, a little hyperbole, but not much.

I guess in the end, *End of a Gun* was another film that I really wanted to like, but ended up a little disappointed, if only because I was looking for something more from my youth. Oh, how I longed for more excitement, more nudity, and dare I say, more of the old Steven Seagal.

–Dean Seyfferle

Cartels (2017)

Cartels should be called *How to Make an Inconsistent Movie*. The first shots of the movie contain news articles, a car on fire, and other images to convey violence with footage of Joe Salazar aka The Great White Shark (Florin Piersic Jr). The film starts off with a shootout with everyone trying to get to Salazar. There are some shots where there is massive blood loss from those that are shot and some where you see no indication of blood. This is actually a problem when Salazar fakes his death with the DEA's help. Before Salazar switches sides, he has a meeting with Sinclaire (Georges St-Pierre). During the raid at Salazar's house, they hide in a room. The sound of Salazar talking while Sinclaire tries to shut him up creates a moment of humor. This scene provides a slight chuckle. Well, the DEA finds them, arrests Sinclaire and shoots Salazar. There is no blood from Salazar's body or any real indication that Joe is dead, because he's not.

It didn't take long for me to call in the director's talent. In the next sequence when they move Salazar's body, they put the body bag down, just to show the audience that Salazar is dead and then they zip it back up. In the world of this film, there is no reason to do this. This is the first of the many times I found myself questioning the director's choices.

The plot takes it's turn when Salazar is alive and goes into hiding. They take him to a hotel, that's open to the public and one of my personal chuckles comes when Maj. Tom Jensen (Luke Goss) points a gun at a bellman and tells him if he moves, he dies. The bellman hangs up the phone, turns around, and drops is cigarette, all which require movement, and it was done fast enough to warrant shooting. This bellman will come back later in the movie, so he had to live, I think it's funny that a character is told not to move and they move.

One of the worst filmed sequences is a clear case of a missing body. There is a scene where there is a fight in the garage, one of the DEA agents gets shot and goes down in the elevator, action cuts to something and then back Jensen and the actors are gone. The plot requires the characters to be gone, but you can't go from laying down in an elevator to nowhere to be seen in less than two seconds. I saw this on my first viewing and it didn't require research. Another sequence that was out of place, was two DEA agents talking about what to do and Salazar puts his suit jacket on in slow motion, there is no reason for it to be slow motion, slow motion indicates closeness to danger, and it made me laugh. You can also see the hotel shootout that some people who have been shot, have fresh blood coming out, while others seem to just lay in a spot where blood used to be as it looked so faded.

The editing of this movie goes from bland to terrible, one sequence as Sinclaire fighting a DEA agent, a sequence I had hope for since it used slow motion appropriately, however it ends with the DEA agent kicking up and it's in a two shot, so the audience sees this kick will miss by miles, he kicks a wall and then all of a sudden just kicks the bad guy. The actor can't defy gravity and kick with both legs. I viewed this sequence a few times just to make sure I didn't miss anything, and I still can't make sense of how he was able to kick him and why the character let the DEA kick him. Also how weak is a wall that one kick breaks part of it off? You can have a much fun making fun of this movie as you do watching it. The only thing that truly bothersome is that the main action takes place in Romania and in particular, in a building called The World Trade Center, which I researched and there is a WTC there, I just think Americans wouldn't appreciate it.

Let's get to the man of the hour, Steven Seagal, plays John Harrison. He authorizes this mission and then spends most the film in present time, while the majority of the film takes place a few days ago. Most of his role is to ask questions to Jensen, which cause him to reflect on it and then we cut to action sequences in the past. It's an oft-used framing device used to covey a possible twist in the movie. It was most effective in films that *Rashomon*. It's not original but it does get Seagal throughout the movie. Seagal's total runtime in the 95-minute movie, is about 15 minutes. The rest is Jensen going over his clusterfuck of a mission. Seagal turns in a largely monotone performance with his constant question asking. There are a couple scenes where he gets angry and stern. He shows his body size in an unfortunate costume decision. When he interviews Jensen in the present day, he wears the tightest leather jacket. When he is in action mode, he wears enough armor that it's okay to look big. You can also put him in loose Hawaiian shirts, which doesn't hide his weight, but he pulls it off. This looked like he was too stubborn to admit he has gained weight and agreed to wear a tight jacket.

It has enough twists and turns to warrant a look. The twists aren't the most original, however it does show that the screenwriter is capable of thinking. It has one of the better endings from Seagal's films, however, *The Usual Suspects* did it much better. When you watch the film in its entirety, and the final twist is revealed, which actually surprised me, you have one final question: wasn't there an easier way?

–Stephen Kessen

China Salesman (2017)

All art is propaganda. However not all propaganda is art. Case in point *China Salesman.*

Seagal. Tyson. Such a billing can only result in an epic-ly cheesy yet entertaining fight movie. Western boxing vs. Eastern karate. Something akin to *Bloodsport* choreography wrapped in an international spy thriller. If you expect this however, you'll be sorely disappointed.

The movie is bad. But not because it features two aging musclemen duking it out with help from CGI and quick cuts. It's bad because it doesn't feature that.

Had *China Salesman* actually been Tyson vs. Seagal. It would have been a blast. Your next guilty pleasure. I know this because within the first ten minutes there is in fact a fight between the two. It's a glorious over-the-top punch fest ending in what is sure to be Mike Tyson's new catch phrase: Now you drink piss, motherfucka." It's the most fun I've had watching a fight since Roddy Piper and Keith David in *They Live.* Tyson even breaks a barrel with a single punch—a huge wooden keg barrel! And then, Seagal all but disappears from the rest of the film. Although he gets significant more screen time, not even Mike Tyson is the star of this movie.

And I use the term 'movie' very loosely. What we get after the action-packed intro is an advertisement. An hour and fifty-minute commercial for the glorious state of China. The plot focuses on a Jian Yan, a telecom vendor salesman for China, and his battle against a corrupt competitor for the first mobile telecom technology contract in Africa. The installation of this telecommunication system could help bring an end to the war-torn country of Uganda. However, the bidding war for the contract is just as fierce and sneaky as the country's in-fighting.

International espionage, romance, civil war… This movie shot for the moon but struck a rock instead. It's hard to decipher Seagal's role in all this. He appears to use his Uganda bar as a front for his gun-selling and mercenary activities. He is recruited by the China Salesman's competitor, an evil European company led by Michael—yeah, I couldn't find his last name, but he's the main villain. Seagal is paid to help disrupt the ability for the China Salesman to win the telecom contract.

Tyson is a former Uganda general, now fighting in the civil war to free his country. He too has been bought by the French villain and assists with political agendas, in-fighting, and corporate sabotage, falsely believing it will help his cause. Meanwhile Michael only cares about winning the telecom contract.

I'm not sure why Mike Tyson's voice is dubbed, especially since he seems to be dubbed by…himself. The dubbing is not as bad as a stereotypical martial arts film from the golden age, but it's also nowhere near as charming as it was in those classics.

The real hero of this advertisement—I mean movie—is China. The China salesman Jian Yan swoops in with honesty and integrity of his homeland to thwart the evil European and bring peace to Uganda. He gets the girl. Lives happily ever after, all while waving the red flag of China high. Literally. There is a scene where rebels are shooting at the Salesman as he attempts to fix desert technology. He is cornered and out of options—but wait…the Chinese flag so close yet so far away. Despite bullets and bombs he's able to break cover and hoist the flag. Through the gun smoke and debris the rebels see the symbol and stop shooting. They hadn't known it was their noble allies from China they were accidentally firing at until the brilliant red was flown.

I love cultural movies that showcase a country's rich heritage, highlighting local customs, art, exploring their fears, struggles, and relevant social issues. Yes, it's possible to do this in action movies. *The China Salesman* does not do this.

Do not waste your time. If you must, watch the first ten minutes and enjoy the single Tyson-Seagal fight scene. Then eat some apple pie and thank God you are not a Chinese citizen.

–Marc Ciccarone

Contract to Kill (2016)

To whom it may concern,

This is my suicide note. If you are reading this, I am dead. The purpose of this letter is to explain why I hung myself from the rafters inside an old closed-down Blockbuster store. The reason is, well...sometimes when a person witnesses an atrocity so horrible and mind-breaking, he can no longer imagine continuing life because he will never be able to unsee the offending incident. So here I am, at the end of my string...er, rope.

What was the horror I witnessed, you ask? It was the 2016 "film" *Contract to Kill*, starring Steven Seagal. It's not even a movie, really. It's just, well, I don't know if a word exists that properly defines what it is, but "shit" comes to mind.

This was the third of three films I was assigned to write about. (The others were *Hard to Kill*, 1990, and *Today You Die*, 2005.) I intentionally chose films from different decades so I could witness Seagal's de-evolution in real time, and man, he looks and acts worse and worse every decade. Today he's just a has-been (or, more accurately, a kind of was) riding on his former (perceived) glories. With *Contract to Kill*, it's obvious that no one, beyond maybe the director, was even trying, least of all Seagal. To say he phoned in his performance would be insulting to Ma Bell. Phone it in? It was more like he used styrofoam cups on the ends of strings to *attempt* to phone it in. He was beyond horrible here. He delivered his dialogue in a manner that gave the impression it took him a lot of effort just to utter words. He almost seemed drunk, slurring the words out. But I don't think he was drunk; I think he just had the most severe case of "don't-give-a-fuck-itis" on record. Seagal seems to be just about the only actor in the film who speaks English as a first language, and somehow he still sounded just as bad speaking it as they do. His stilted delivery is reminiscent of the way the computer in *War Games* speaks. Beyond his apparent difficulty in merely speaking, Seagal refuses to exert himself even the tiniest bit. And that includes the fight scenes, which are ridiculously lazy.

Seagal wasn't the only actor giving a bad performance either. *Contract to Kill* is filled with them. While Keoni Waxman's script is really, really awful (it felt like they were winging it as they made the movie), his direction is easily the best thing about the movie. Thanks to him, *Contract to Kill* looks like a really slick infomercial that could almost manage to keep you awake for five minutes at three in the morning. If aliens came to earth and watched *Contract to Kill* to learn what an action movie was, they'd leave believing the purpose of an action movie was to put viewers to sleep.

So little effort was put into *Contract to Bore* that you would be tempted to believe it was actually made for some duplicitous reason such as laundering drug money or to be someone's tax write-off. The plot deals with a Mexican cartel and "radical Islamic terrorists" (a right-wing catchphrase to remind us that Seagal is an ultra-ultra-ultra-right-winger, just to the right of Genghis Khan) form an alliance. Seagal, a former CIA/FBI/ Navy seal/whatever/who gives a shit, is tapped to recruit his own team to stop them. The team he selects is hardly the Expendables. He gets to pick anyone in the world, so he of course selects a guy whose specialty is flying drones and a sexy young woman who weighs roughly 100 pounds. And in true Seagal fashion, we are told that the young woman is his character's ex-girlfriend—a detail that requires more suspension of disbelief than anything else in this ridiculous production. If you believe Seagal and his two cohorts probably wouldn't be enough to stop these guys, think again, because they also have their own jet! Yes, that's right, their own jet. It doesn't do anything special though; it's just a regular old run of the mill jet. (I envision Seagal doing weird sex stuff to his ex-girlfriend—yuck for her—and eating a variety of confections up in the sky inside his sweet jet.)

And just in case the movie didn't suck enough before, Seagal delivers a long-winded right-wing political lecture about how the Obama administration was supposedly kissing the asses of terrorists, yadda yadda yadda. I'm certain this scene gave Seagal raging wood that was as big a hard-on as he is.

When I got finished with the movie, I felt sick to my stomach. Remembering that induced vomiting can sometimes make a person feel better, I stuck my fingers down my throat and went to town, to no avail. But as I hunkered over the toilet, staring down at my floating vomit, I realized that that vomit had significantly more acting ability than Steven Seagal. This isn't to say it had any at all. No, it had zero talent, but that was still more than Seagal.

I remember when I was younger and my best friend and I went to see *On Deadly Ground* at the theater. That movie was so bad that we laughed and laughed at its stupidity. (That was the first really bad Seagal movie, in my estimation; one of the clunkers that would ultimately earn him a one-way ticket to direct-to-DVD Land.) I would have never envisioned a day when Seagal movies had sunk so low that I would actually look back on that turd fondly, but that day is here.

So anyway, I've committed suicide. I'm dead now. There are a lot of things I'll miss about life, but Steven Seagal movies will not be one of them.

–Andrew J. Rausch

Attrition (2018)

Growing up I was a fan of martial arts movies. It didn't matter if it was Bruce Lee, Chuck Norris, Steven Seagal, or even Jean Claude Van Damme. I even devoured movies that were comedy and had little value or true talent. I was excited initially about a project centered around the movies of Seagal. Unfortunately, the movies I so enjoyed growing up in the 80s and 90s were already taken. The movie available to review was *Attrition* from 2018. The movie was written and produced by Seagal. The basic premise is that Seagal, who is also the star of the movie, is an ex-special forces operative turned doctor and martial artist. He is an expat, named Axe, aka "The Wild One," who has converted to Buddhism and has moved to Thailand. He is beloved by the people in his village.

I got lost along the way and tried to watch the movie twice. I did not understand the scenes where Seagal was in bed and a girl began appearing to him. At first, I assumed it was his nurse and then it morphed into an angel of sorts. He questioned her appearance and she mentioned that she did not have to answer him because she would come to him.

Axe seems to be the one the people in the village turn to when things go bad, not just medically but when someone is messing with them. Which brings us to the part I understand. A man owes a considerable amount of money to a local drug lord and mentions that there is a beautiful girl in his village. He trades her for his money because she is believed to have special powers. She is able to dream walk with Seagal and when she is confronted by the kingpin, she speaks to them telepathically. This backfires on her as she realizes that the kingpin is neither worried nor afraid of the fact, she has mystic powers. He is intrigued and is desperate to have her under his control. The father then pleads with Axe for his help. He finally agrees and he calls out to his former team members. He also calls a fellow student of his master. They make a plan to get inside the special club where the girl is possibly held.

The movie is extremely slow and there is no character development. Even though, at one time I was a great fan of Seagal, I was not drawn into the movie at all. I could understand the urgency that the characters needed in saving the girl, Tara, from getting raped and held hostage by the head of the gang. One minute you see a kidnapping, then guns blazing, and suddenly Seagal is praying in a cave. The transition between scenes is also off. As the scene is a couple minutes in before you realize that they forgot to put 'three years later' to show the passing of time. It is tossed in almost as an afterthought.

The concept of a foreigner in an exotic land, being adored by the locals, and then heroically saving a local girl is a common trope in action movies. Stallone even did the same thing with the first *Expendables* movies. However, Stallone took the time to show that each character, played by a notable actor, had their own distinct personalities.

It shares a commonality with the Jean Claude Van Damme movie, *Kickboxer*. A foreigner determined to do right by a kidnapped girl being tortured by the evil master mind and his champion fighter where Seagal has a kidnapped girl with supernatural powers kidnapped by a drug king pin. There is a hint of a possibility of a romance between the characters Axe and Tara. Yet, with *Kickboxer* you have the opportunity to become emotionally involved with the character as he is forced to witness his villain intentionally harm his brother.

All of these elements are sorely missing from what could be an excellent movie. A psychic girl in the hands of a criminal mastermind and you have only one person with the background to save her? If I knew what the point was, I might care. Is he just a sick man who wants to rape and torture her or does he also want to use her powers for his own twisted purposes? With the sound quality less than optimal if the villain's motivations were explained, it was not offered in the subtitles, so I assume it was English and I missed it.

Just when the action starts to take place, it is over in the blink of an eye. There is no explanation of the girl's wellbeing, if they truly won, or if the girl was simply rescued. What it wraps up with is Seagal spending most of his time with a speech about the study of martial arts, the problems with the modern system of teaching, the importance of linage, protection of the innocent, etc. As a former student and fan of the martial arts, this is the only point of the movie that I understood.

Lastly, you see Seagal sing and play guitar at his friend's karaoke bar while his teammates who rescued the girl party in the crowd. It leaves me wondering if the whole point of this movie was to waste production dollars for the last two or three minutes of the movie, to deliver an important message about the studying of martial arts, (almost a direct word for word rip off of what Bruce Lee spent his whole short life preaching), and to give a vehicle to bolster his own musical career.

Personally, I was left feeling disappointed and annoyed by the fact that this movie was nothing more than a waste of time and glad that Showtime had a free trial, so I did not have to waste money, too.

–Kristina Stancil

General Commander (2019)

I was fortunate enough to grow up in the golden era of Modern Action Movies. I was a teenager in the years 1987-1994, during which time *Die Hard*, *Terminator 2: Judgement Day*, *Predator*, *Rambo III*, *Total Recall*, and many other machismo-filled bloodfests raked in huge box office receipts. Even Sensei Seagal had SIX hit films during this span of time. I ate them up - the explosions, the guns, the catchphrases, the tough guys blowing up all the scary bad guys; it was all magical and exciting to me. That is, until l started to see the lines and color-by-numbers underneath the image. I started to be able to predict the action, and the notes of the movie; here's where we meet the team in the movie; the wise-cracking second banana, the asshole that's going to end up betraying everyone; here's where they take the mission that goes wrong and one of the favorite (but still secondary) characters die, and so on. One puts away childish things when they become a man, so when *Pulp Fiction* showed up in 1994 it blew my 20-year old, no-longer teenage mind. I thought there was no way I could ever be surprised by a dumb old action movie ever again. Boy, was I wrong.

Leave it to Sensei to take on the lead role in this adventurous reimagining of the formulaic action film, *General Commander*. The title - is that a military rank of some kind? NOPE. It's the name of the business he starts around halfway through the movie. Oh, so they explain the meaning of the name, right? NOPE. But's that's not even REMOTELY the most confusing thing about this film. The movie starts with Sensei's character, Jake Alexander, being grilled by the Hillary Clinton-esque director of the CIA. "Jake Alexander" seems like a very all-American quarterback kind of a name, which is unfortunate, since Seagal looks more like a 17th century Eastern European vampire in this movie. But I digress. She wants to know if he killed Orsetti. Who's this Orsetti? DID he kill him? Before you can get too involved in these questions, the editors introduce flashes, noises, and short, nonsensical cuts and changes of perspective and focus. I started to wonder if "I think I might be having a stroke" is an acceptable aesthetic choice in film.

Fortunately, an onscreen infographic appears (God knows, I love me a good infographic in an action movie). It tells us all about the blackmarket organ trade. I guess that's what the movie is about? Quick cut, and a graphic on the screen lets us know it's TWO WEEKS EARLIER and we're in Cambodia in the middle of some kind of operation with Jake and…his team, I guess? There are people on the screen, and it *seems* like we should know who they are. *Jesus, DID I have a stroke?* There's a bunch of blandly good-looking people and a smart-assed Australian guy(?) that turn out to be a team working with Jake to bust an organ smuggling ring. One of them gets killed in the operation, and the movie spends the next 10-15 minutes *really* milking it - we should *really* care about this person that we literally just met and whose name I didn't even know until after he was dead. I still don't know anyone's name, really. There's been at least 12 significant characters introduced and I know 4 people's names. Holy shit, I'm 40 minutes into the movie already? "WHAT'S GOING ON?", I yell out to no one in the quiet of my apartment. After 15 minutes mourning a character that apparently appeared from the ether without any scintilla of a backstory, suddenly Jake is <u>IN DANGER!!!</u> A new character named Hayes has appeared and hired another guy to find and kill Jake. Why? Who knows?

About two-thirds of the way into the film, the writers (in a brilliant meta/fourth wall breaking moment) realize that we *still don't know* the names of about 75% of the characters. So, they start using names A LOT. It doesn't matter really, they need to wrap this story up and get it in under an hour thirty, so blah blah blah, they set the trap for the bad guy, there's a big fight, they blow up a helicopter with a rocket launcher and the smart mouthed Australian guy from before says "Merry Christmas, *motherfucker!*" Catchphrase? I guess. There's a car crash with an unreasonably large explosion, in which the bad guy is hobbled and gimps away from the burning car. To illustrate the deep heroism of the main character, I quote from the Wikipedia plot summary for the film; "Alexander swiftly kills a struggling Orsetti". Ah yes, because nothing says hero like "swiftly killing" a "struggling" villain. Credits roll? Oh no, not yet. First, Jake has to go…home? To his…wife? Maybe? Who knows? Suddenly, our old friend HAYES returns, this time with a drone which drops a bomb on Jake's…house, maybe? And he…dies?

In the Grateful Dead song "Scarlet Begonias," Jerry Garcia sings that "Once in a while you get shown the light/ In the strangest of places if you look at it right." On the surface, it would be easy to misunderstand this film as a shitty, microcosmically-budgeted direct-to-video action movie with no brain or heart. But maybe, *just maybe*, this movie is a work of accidental genius that lays bare all of the truths of the absurdity of the modern age. Combat as a faceless, confusing melee where names or personalities have no value or meaning. The world as a cruel, remorseless trap in which mortal enemies can appear out of nowhere and for no apparent reason. Time is meaningless. We yell into the void. And death awaits all. Maybe we <u>are</u> having a stroke - a stroke of Dadaist genius.

–Daryl Bean

Beyond the Law (2019)

One assumes, going into a Steven Seagal film, that the great wooden one will be the character with whom our loyalty as an audience lies. However, the 2019 action-revenge drama, *Beyond the Law,* keeps us wondering. As it unfolds, it seems to want to be an examination of the nature of loyalty. But the film itself never decides who or what it wants to be loyal to, shedding more confusion than clarity on the theme.

Indeed, it feels like we are watching two movies whose plots happen to collide in the end. One is a Charles Bronson-style revenge drama. The other, a brooding end-of-the-road drama about a retired mob boss. Neither story is particularly developed, compelling, or inventive.

It goes something like this:

A pair of mobsters come to party boy Chance Wilson's (Chester Rushing) shit-hole apartment looking for gambling debts owed. The money is not recovered, and he is shot in the head by the lead mobster, Desmond (Zack Ward). His partner holds Chance's head up by the hair, seemingly unafraid that the bullet might also hit his hand. He knew where the special effects department placed the squib, I suppose.

But this late party-animal was the son of Frank Wilson (Johnny Messner), a retired cop who now lives in a cabin in the wilderness. While on the job, he was the kind of cop that current efforts to reform the police reform are aimed at. But all of his corrupt acts, of course, were in the name of justice when his hands were tied by official red tape.

Frank arrives at the big city and pretty soon tracks down Charlotte (Saxon Sharbino), a girl Chance was hot for. It seems she was the one who stole the money that Chance had hidden for his gambling debts. Even though she got his son killed, Frank leaves her with the warning that the people who killed Chance will not stop looking for that money.

Meanwhile, reformed mob boss Finn (Steven Seagal) is visited by Johnny and finds some kind of empathy for another long-suffering father. Finn, you see, is the father of Desmond, who pulled the trigger on Chance.

Finn warns his son to stop hanging out with his criminal pals (unaware that Desmond himself is their leader, following in daddy's footsteps). Finn suspects that Desmond is lying, and actually did kill Chance, though he denies it to the old man's face.

Frank keeps looking for, and knocking off, members of the gang in one clichéd action set-piece after another. Finally, he sends Desmond across the Rainbow Bridge.

But then comes the inevitable showdown between the two diabolical daddies. Seagal kicks Messner's ass without even stooping or breaking a sweat. We know he won't allow himself to lose a screen fight. But the joke is on him. Frank has called 911, and the sirens are on their way.

As a coda, in case you think Charlotte got away with the cash, she is murdered by Karina (Yulia Klass), another shady woman with ties to the criminal gang.

It's pretty hard to take any of this seriously, though its deadly serious tone wants us to think its an important study of the dark side of humanity. We know that from the first shot of gangsters pulling up to a shabby building in a tilted "Dutch angle," just so we know it's stylish and dark. For the rest of its 91 minutes, however, we are given no more hints that anybody considered anything about style, least of all director James Cullen Bressack.

For the first half of this movie we are certain that Frank is the main character. The plot really hinges on his search for his son's killer. Seagal's Finn seems to be a sub-plot. We see him infrequently, to offer advice or to fill in a minor plot point. Then, in the end, we are expected as an audience to switch loyalties and side with Finn because he doesn't actively participate in crime and murder anymore after a lifetime of it.

We feel dirty siding with Frank. The same goes with Finn, and, frankly, with all the characters in this movie. None of them has a moral center. There is not one soul worth rooting for, though the film wants us to forgive the heinous transgressions of Frank and Chance because they are daddies who love their twisted sons. But the sons are both following in the footsteps of their younger, less grounded daddies, so who is really to blame here?

The movie strenuously sidesteps morality at every turn by refusing to dig beneath the surface of any action or character.

The dialogue is serviceable at best, but often borders on the laughable. Here is a choice snippet: "Sometimes when a man is hard to find, it's 'cause he didn't want to be found." – I guess that adds up, but duh.

As for the performances, most of them are adequate, and there is no standout, unless it is Bill Cobbs as Swilley, Frank's neighbor in his wilderness home. He is a minor character, but he would be the film's sole redeemable one, were it not for him eventually ratting out Frank to the mobsters.

But it's Seagal's performance we are concerned with here, isn't it? The great wooden thespian does not disappoint. He is a towering, fat old man with dye hair and the swagger of a lean cage fighter. He delivers every single line in the exact same whispered monotone.

Seagal seems to be hoping we won't notice that there is no passion behind any line delivery if he underplays it enough. He also seems to be attempting a southern accent, just like a real actor, bless his heart. But the accent is barely noticeable, and at times, it disappears entirely.

Beyond the Law is perhaps an appropriate title for a movie that has no moral center and no respect for any rule of law. It is a confused mishmash of action movie tropes, to which nobody seems invested to any degree beyond a paycheck.

–Ron Ford

The Authors

Jon Arking *(aka Jon King)* is a Michigan-based broadcaster and journalist with over 35 years of experience. He has authored two children's books, *Ishkadoodle: A Boy, His Vacuum & Their Outerspace Adventure* and *Ishkadoodle & The 8 Planets of Hanukkah*. He is also the co-author of *Hot Mess* and the upcoming *Grounds*.

Hall CF Astell is a critic, author, publisher, and film festival director who runs the Apocalypse Later Empire from his lair in Phoenix, AZ. He has six books in print through Apocalypse Later Press. *Apocalypse Later Reviews* will celebrate its fifteenth anniversary in 2022. The Apocalypse Later International Fantastic Film Festival (ALIFFF) is in its sixth year. He brings quality films to new eyeballs at conventions across the southwest through the Apocalypse Later Roadshow. His website is apocalypselaterempire.com.

Daryl Bean lives, works, and does things in relative anonymity and is totally fine with that. He'd put his website address here, but he doesn't have one.

Kurt "Thunderlord" Belcher lives in the mythical kingdom of Kentucky. He must continually dodge Bloody Thraborlaxes and Golden Shlob Bœars to make his way to the market at Neckboneton to sell his ridiculous paper scribbles. He likes dogs.

Chris Brown is a longtime film fan and budding action movie star. He is the proprietor of Comics and More in Madison Heights, MI.

John Bruske is a co-host to many podcasts, including the *Jean Pod Van Dammecast*, *Rage in a Cage*, and *Everyday I'm Russellin'*. When not trying to completely watch the Canon Films filmography, he spends time with his family and working on intellectual properties.

With his love of action cinema beginning with multiple VHS viewings of *Robocop* & *The Terminator* as an 8-year-old, Scottish born **Aaron Carruthers** combines his knowledge of cinema and passion for film journalism.

Paul Celano is a nerd born and raised in Michigan. He is an artist and loves to make people laugh. He is a huge movie buff, good and bad. His favorite genre of movie is horror coming in all shapes and sizes.

Marc Ciccarone is the co-owner of Blood Bound Books, an independent publisher specializing in dark fiction. They offer a wide variety of novels, anthologies, coloring books, and horror-themed greeting cards. He is also a co-founder of The Splatter Club, an online community for readers and authors of extreme and bizarro fiction. Connect with him at bloodgutsandstory.com

Michael Cieslak is a lifetime reader and writer of horror, mystery, and speculative fiction. He is an officer in the Great Lakes Association of Horror Writers and is the editor of the *Erie Tales* anthologies. His works have appeared in a number of collections including *DOA: Extreme Horror, Dead Science, Vicious Verses and Reanimated Rhymes*, the GLAHW anthologies, *Alter Egos* Vol 1., and the collaborative steampunk novel *Army of Brass*. *Urbane Decay*, a collection of Michael's short fiction, was released in 2018 by Source Point Press. Michael is the Editor in Chief of Dragon's Roost Press and his mental excreta, including his personal blog *They Napalmed My Shrubbery This Morning*, can be found on-line at thedragonsroost.net.

Paul Counelis is a freelance writer (*Rue Morgue, Scary Monsters, Fear Finder, Fright Times*), author (*Evil World Outside, 25 Underrated Horror Films and 'The Exorcist', The Greatest Horror Movie Ever Made*) and member of the Flint Horror Collective hailing from urban, renegade Flint, Michigan. As Uncle Salem he is the voice of horror punks LORDS OF OCTOBER and the host of a weekly online radio show, *Blank Generation with Uncle Salem.*

Todd Davidson is the co-host of *The Basement Fodder Podcast* and founder of Basement of Doom productions. For the last ten years he has been reviewing comics, films and pop culture on podcasts with listeners in 17 countries.

Jeff Dolniak is an enigma wrapped in a damp hanky. Over the past 45 years, Jeff has strived for mediocrity with acting roles in cult films such as *Blown, Desert Man Beast* and *Sportkill*. Cult film aficionados may also know him as the creator of the popular DVD series, *42nd Street Forever*. Currently he churns out news and reviews for Cinema Head Cheese.

Ron Ford is an actor, writer and filmmaker from the Seattle area. In 1994, after moving to LA, he sold his first screenplay, which became the horror hit, *The Fear*. He became a filmmaker in 1997 with his directorial debut, *Alien Force*, starring Burt Ward of Batman fame. He became a gun for hire for film distributors, who could be relied upon to deliver salable movies on budget and on schedule. He produced, wrote and directed more than a dozen genre titles, including *Hollywood Mortuary, Tiki, Mark of Dracula* and *Witchcraft XI: Sisters in Blood*. As an actor, he can be seen in the movies *Home of the Brave, Killer Tomatoes Eat France*, and many others, as well as on the TV shows *Z Nation, The Young Riders, Two Busy Debras* and *Hey, Dude*. In 2003 he moved to Spokane, WA where he continues to live and work.

David C. Hayes is an author, performer, filmmaker and academic. Visit him online at www.davidchayes.com.

Kent Hill is a screenwriter, author, publisher and podcaster. First published in the United States in 2013 by StrangeHouse Books, Hill would go on to write numerous novellas and short stories published individually and in a variety of anthologies. He currently has screenplays in development and is a writer of upcoming films from Rene Perez at www.thedarkestmachines.com. He lives on 'The Downs' in Queensland, Australia with his wife and son.

J. R. Jordan has been writing about Hollywood for several years. He is the author of *Showmanship: The Cinema of William Castle* and *Robert Wise: The Motion Pictures*.

Pat Kawula is a writer, editor, and curator of the award-winning comic anthology *Get in the Game* published by Source Point Press. When he is not hiding under his desk suffering from an incurable case of Imposter Syndrome, he will peek out to write something witty. This bio is NOT one of those times... although maybe it is. Who knows?

Stephen Kessen was born July of 1989 in Cincinnati Ohio. He recently earned his master's degree from Regent University with a focus on Directing and Producing. He writes screenplays, directs movies, and acts with his film *Moving Ashley* winning over a dozen awards from various festivals across the world. When he's not working in the performing arts, he can be found reading murder mystery novels, traveling, and playing with his two cats, Chloe and Tybalt.

Joshua "Samurai" Knode is a Do-goooder, Righter of Wrongs, Champion of the Little Guy, and all-around badass. He is the author of *Second Sun, Obsidian Road* and *True: A Gunslinger's Tale* and host of the podcast *Samurai Says*. He lives in Ohio with one cat, his brother and an embarrassingly large collection of vintage playing cards.

Joe LaLonde is an award-winning blogger who loves to combine his love for movies and his desire to see people grow their leadership abilities. He writes about leadership at https://jmlalonde.com and has released a book titled *Reel Leadership* which can be found wherever books are sold.

Corey Maslowski considers himself a connoisseur of terrible movies and TV series, and loves adding that charm and flair to his work. Born and raised in Northern Michigan, he is best known for his work on the story "Logging Out" in the comic anthology *Get in the Game* as well as pieces featured in the collection *Theater of the Mind*.

Kevin Moyers is an author and podcaster who feels fully vindicated in choosing Jean Claude Van Damme in the "Who would win a fight?" argument way back in the 1990s.

Jeff O'Brien is a prolific author of strange fiction and musician. Among his many works include The Bigboobenstein series, Goth Queen, Blood Orgy in the Woods, House of the Blood Nymphs, Sisters of Manchester, and many, many more. He is a staunch advocate of trans rights and trans equality, supports Black Lives Matter, and donates to Planned Parenthood. He doesn't very much like cops or any other authority figure but loves coffee and cats.

Christoph Paul is an author and songwriter. He is the managing editor of CLASH Books, an independent literary press focusing on fiction, non-fiction, poetry, & art that blends & challenges genre expectations (www.clashbooks.com) and the editor of CLASH Media.

Charles E. Pratt, Jr. is a writer of film criticism and longtime movie fan. His work has appeared in *The 101 Scariest Movies Ever Made* and he is the co-author of *The Cinematic Misadventures of Ed Wood*, both from Bear Manor Media.

Andrew J. Rausch is a film journalist and the author of more than fifty books. This includes such titles as *The Cinematic Misadventures of Ed Wood* (w/ Charles E. Pratt Jr.), *The Films of Martin Scorsese and Robert De Niro*, and *My Best Friend's Birthday: The Making of a Quentin Tarantino Film*. He writes for numerous publications and is an online editor for *Diabolique* magazine. He lives with his wife and children in Independence, Kansas.

Michael Rizzo is an award winning, Detroit-based filmmaker and creator. He is the owner of the production company, Broken Multiverse.

Jed Rowen is an actor living in Los Angeles who's hoping to audition for the next Steven Seagal movie.

A P Sessler, a resident of North Carolina's Outer Banks, wishes he could stick to walls and jump trees without the aid of wires while fighting

50 bad guys at once. His all-time favorite martial arts film is the Shaw Brothers' *Five Elements Ninjas* aka *Chinese Super Ninjas*.

Dean Seyfferle is a video producer and content creator with over twenty-five years' experience. He currently lives in Arizona with his wife, stepdaughter, and an amassment of domestic animals.

Kristina Stancil has been writing since she was very young. Her first publication was shortly after turning 18 in a short interview with Hall of Fame wrestler, Ric Flair. Since then, she has worked as a freelance sports consultant for the *Houma Daily Courier*, an entertainment consultant for the *Bayou Gumbo Entertainment* guide, and, most recently, was the New Orleans Horror Movie Examiner. Kristina is the author of the *Fox Inc* series, *Shades of Me* (poetry collection), *Eddie the Monkey* (a children's book), and an editor and contributor to the *Serial Thrillerz Ezine*. In addition to her several titles, Kristina is the owner of Blood Reign Lit Magazine, specializing in the publication of new horror writers.

Montilee Stormer is a horror writer, film reviewer, and podcaster who never expected to actually live the inescapable horror of a Steven Segal movie. She now silently weeps for what could have been, but feel free to Google her name and despair along with her.

William Tea doesn't know aikido, but he does know how to write scary stories, as well as the occasional cult film review. Stalk him online at williamtea.com.

Michael Vaughn is a film critic/historian and the author of *The Ultimate Guide to Strange Cinema* from Schiffer Publishing. Their other credits include AMC's *The Bite, Films in Review,* and *Scream Magazine*.

Greg Wright holds a Ph.D. in Contemporary American Literature and Film from Michigan State University, and he has published academic analyses of popular culture as well as creative writing in fiction, nonfiction, and graphic novels. His comic book writing includes the pulp-fueled *Wild Bullets*, the steampunk mashup *Monstrous*, the satirical fantasy *Claim: A Song of Ire and Vice*, and the *Holliston* graphic novels, based on Adam Green's cult favorite horror sitcom. His *TABLOID!* novel series follows a mother-daughter team of paranormal investigative journalists.

Tony Doug Wright is a writer of comics and a graphic novel for Source Point Press. He's a husband, father, historian, lost soul of rock and roll, and a true crime writer-in-training.

Scott Bradley is the author of a novel, *The Dark*, and editor of *The Book of Lists Horror* and *Explosions: Stories of Our Landmined World*, a charity anthology for Mines Advisory Group. His journalism and criticism has appeared in *The Kansas City Star* and *Film Quarterly*, and most recently he penned an adaptation of Joe Lansdale's story "Duck Hunt" for the comics anthology *God of the Razor*. Scott currently lives in Southwest Missouri.

Kieran Fisher is a big fan of action movies, schlock horror, giant monsters, and crime sagas. In addition to Diabolique, he also writes for Arrow Video and Film School Rejects.

Christopher Smith started writing short stories as a way to pass his lunch hour at work, not realizing how deep the roots of this pastime would grow. He experiments with many different genres and styles. He lives in Michigan with his wife, three children, and five (million) cats.